Boadicea Haranguing the Britons, courtesy of the National Portrait Gallery

Nearly two thousand years ago a terrible disaster occurred in Britain.

Three cities were sacked, eighty thousand Romans and their allies perished and the island was nearly freed from Rome. Moreover, all this ruin was brought upon the Romans by a woman, a fact which caused them great shame. The person who was chiefly instrumental in rousing the natives and persuading them to fight the Romans, who was thought worthy to be their leader, and who directed the conduct of the entire war, was Boudica, a British woman of the royal family of an East Anglian tribe who possessed above average intelligence.

And the author Cassius Dio added: -

'In stature she was very tall, in appearance most terrifying, in the glance of her eye most fierce, and her voice was harsh; a great mass of the tawniest hair fell to her hips; around her neck was a large golden necklace; and she wore a tunic of divers colours over which a thick mantle was fastened with a brooch. This was her invariable attire.'

Lucius Cassius Dio, Roman History (LXII.1-2)

The RIDDLE of BOUDICA

Essex Hundred Publications
Benfleet
Essex
www.essex100.com
ask@essex100.com

The Riddle of Boudica

First published November 2022
Andrew Summers
© Andrew Summers
November 2022
All rights reserved

No part of this book may be reprinted or reproduced or utilised in any form or by any electronic, mechanical or other means, now known or hereafter invented, including photocopying and recording, or in any information storage or retrieval system, without the permission in writing from the publishers.

A catalogue record for this book is available from
The British Library
ISBN 9780993108334

Typeset by Hutchins Creative
Printed by 4edge Publishing
22 Eldon Way
Eldon Way Industrial Estate
Hockley Essex SS5 4AD

Contents

Acknowledgements

In bringing this book to publication I have benefited greatly from the valuable resources held by Essex Libraries, the Essex Records Office, Colchester Castle Museum, and the Verulamium Museum (St Albans).

Additionally I would like to thank Liz Barham and the team of osteologists at the Museum of London Archaeology (MOLA) for their excellent observations on bone decomposition.

Reviewing the original Roman authors, Tacitus and Dio, the sources of the story of Boudica is not only confusing but time consuming. On this matter I am indebted to Margaret Hughes, of the Atherstone Civic Society, for many clarifications of Latin to English translations, to Joshua J. Mark of the *World History Encyclopedia* and Professor Richard Hingley, the Professor of Archaeology at the University of Durham. Additional thanks are given to Zofia Matyjaszkiewicz for a potted history of the Roman Baths in Bath and to Paul Lind, the Town Serjeant of Colchester Borough Council, for showing me round the Moot Hall and the Council Chamber.

Specials thanks are due to John Debenham for creating the index and text checking and to Glenis Summers for proof reading.

Trying to verify facts from nearly 2,000 years ago is a considerable challenge and I can only hope the reader is not disappointed with the results and conclusions made.

For errors made I offer humble apologies and as ever comments are always welcome.

Andrew Summers

Some Useful Definitions

Civitas A Small tribal community.

Consul A holder of high (Roman) political office with defined responsibilities for a set time period.

Gnaeus, Gneus, Publius
For much of Roman history, these were common Roman Latin praenomens, or personal first names, widely used during the time of the Republic or Empire. For the Roman individuals noted in the book the personal first names have been omitted to avoid confusion.

Legion The principal unit of the Roman army comprising 3000 to 6000 infantry and light cavalry. The legion was usually added to by the Auxilia or Auxiliaries, non-Roman citizens who provided extra horse soldiers or who had specialist skills such as archery which in turn brought the legions' numbers up to around 10,000.

Pax Romana The peaceful coexistence between the local tribes and the authorities of the Roman Empire.

Opidium A defended or fortified administrative centre or town.

Veni, vidi, vici *I came; I saw; I conquered* a phrase attributed to Julius Caesar from his first invasion of Britain in 55BC but used earlier after his victory at Zile in Turkey over Pharnaces II, King of Pontus in 47BC.

Vexillation A company of Roman troops under one vexillum, (the standard bearing the emblem and name of the parent legion) and detached for special service from a main body of soldiers.

Illustrations and Maps

All images from the Essex Hundred Collection
except where noted above.

Every effort has been made to contact copyright holders of images reproduced in this book. If any have been inadvertently overlooked the publisher will be pleased to make restitution at the earliest opportunity

English and Roman Place Names

English name	Roman (Latin) name
British Isles	Britannia
Anglesey	Mona
Caistor St. Edmunds	Venta Icenorum
Cambridge	Duroliponte
Canterbury	Durovernum Cantiacorum
Dunstable	Durocobrivis
Chelmsford	Caesaromagus
Chester	Deva
Colchester	Camulodunum
Exeter	Isca Dumnoniorum
France	Gaul
Gloucester	Glevum
Godmanchester	Durovigutum
High Cross	Venonis
Leicester	Ratae Coritoranum
Mancetter	Manduessedum
Lincoln	Lindum
London	Londininium
Silchester	Calleva Atrebatum
St Albans	Verulamium
Wales	Cambria
Wroxeter	Virconium
York	Eboracum

Please note original spelling of Latin place names varies according to source

Tribal Map of England and Wales AD 43

Tribal Territories

(*see map inside page 12*)

England

Iceni	(Norfolk, Suffolk, Lincolnshire, Essex) King Prasutagus Queen Boudica
Catuvellauni	(Hertfordshire, Cambridgeshire, Bedfordshire) King Cunobelinus / Cunobelin (Cymbeline) The Catuvellauni ruled over the Trinovantes Cunobelinus died and his kingdom was divided between his two sons Togodumnus and Caratacus
Trinovantes	(London, Essex, Suffolk, Cambridgeshire)
Brigantes	(Yorkshire, Lancashire) King Venutius Queen Cartimandua
Atrebates	(Hampshire, West Sussex)
Cantiaci	(Kent)

Wales

Silures	(South and East Wales)
Ordovices	(Central and North Wales)
Degeangli	North Wales and Flintshire

The above is not a comprehensive list of all the English and Welsh tribes in 43AD. Only those involved during the Boudica rebellion are noted above. Tribal boundaries tended to change and overlap.

English Tribal Leaders

	Born	Death
Catuvellauni		
Cassivellaunus		
hunted by Julius Caesar during first invasion	unknown	after 54BC
Cunobelinus. (Cymbeline)	unknown	AD42
Togodumnus		
(1st son of Cunobelinus) Died of wounds during AD 43 invasion	unknown	AD43
Caratacus (2nd son of Cunobelinus) Captured by the Romans	unknown	after AD50 in Rome
Adminius A son of Cunobelinus or possibly a brother in law of Togodumnus	unknown	after AD45
Brigantes		
Queen Cartimandua Responsible for handing over Caratacus to the Romans	unknown	after AD69
Iceni		
Boudica	unknown	AD60 or 61
King Prasutagus	unknown	AD58

Principal Romans

Julias Caesar 100BC - 44BC

Led invasions of Britain in 55 and 54BC.
He left after short campaigns.
Assassinated 15 March 44 BC in Rome.

Emperors Served

Augustus	27BC - 14AD
Tiberius	14AD - 37AD
Caligula	37AD - 41AD

Claudius 41AD - 54AD

Nearly 100 years after Caesar, Claudius invaded Britain in AD 43 with four legions. The *Colonia of Claudia Victricensis* was established as the provincial capital of Britannia at Camulodunum (Colchester) where a large Temple was dedicated in his honour.
He died in October 54AD suspected of being poisoned.

Nero 54AD - 68AD

At the age of 17 Nero became Emperor following the death of his uncle Claudius. Nero oversaw the revolt of Queen Boudica. In later years, following the murder of his mother, Nero's rule became erratic and unpredictable and he committed suicide.

Roman Governors | **Years in post**

Roman Governors	Years in post
Aulus Plautius	AD43 - AD47
Ostorious Scapula	AD47 - AD52
Didius Gallus	AD52 - AD57
Quintus Veranius	AD57
Suetonius Paulinus	AD57 - AD62
Publius Petronius Turpilianus	AD62 - AD63
Trebillus Maximus	AD63 - AD69
Julius Agricola	AD77 - AD84

Procurators

Catus Decianus	AD59 - AD61
Julius Alpinus Classicianus	AD61 - AD65

Writers

	Born - Died
Cornelius Tacitus	AD56 - AD120
Lucius Cassius Dio	AD155 - AD235

Roman Legions and Commanders during Boudica's Revolt

Legion and base	Commander
II Legion (Gloucester)	Poenius Postumus
IX Legion (Lincoln)	Petilius Cerialis
XIV, XX	Suetonius Paulinus Governor

Introduction

This book is about the short lived Boudican revolt of AD 60/61. To put the revolt into context it is necessary to examine the period just before Julius Caesar's first incursion into the British Isles in BC55 and continue through to AD65, a period of about 120 years.

The Rebellion of Queen Boudica, or Boadicea, against the Roman occupiers was nearly 2000 years ago. After early success, the revolt was decisively crushed and the Romans remained in Britain for at least another 350 years. Despite the blood and fury, Boudica's efforts played no part in getting the Romans to leave. The Romans only left the British Isles when the Roman Empire collapsed at its centre and not because of Boudica.

During the 350-year Roman occupation there were several rebellions from the 'natives' notably by the Welsh tribes and northern Brigantes between AD 71 and 78. Forty years later the Brigantes rose in revolt again and defeated the IX Legion at York. In AD 185 part of the occupying Roman Army mutinied and eleven years later much of northern England, York and Chester were overrun by marauders from Scotland. In AD 286 the Roman Commander of the British fleet, Marcus Aurelius Carausius, proclaimed himself Emperor of an independent Britain. Seven years later he was murdered by his finance minister Allectus on the orders of Julius Constantius, the Roman Emperor. The insurrections were supressed, the mutiny put down, the usurpers overthrown and Roman rule returned to more or less normal.

Yet, despite all the upheavals in the British Isles during Rome's long tenure, it is only Boudica who is especially remembered, particularly so in the English towns of Colchester and St Albans. Of course in London too, there is Thomas Thornycroft's iconic sculpture of Boadicea riding her chariot which stands outside the Houses of Parliament on the Embankment in Westminster.

The Roman Empire

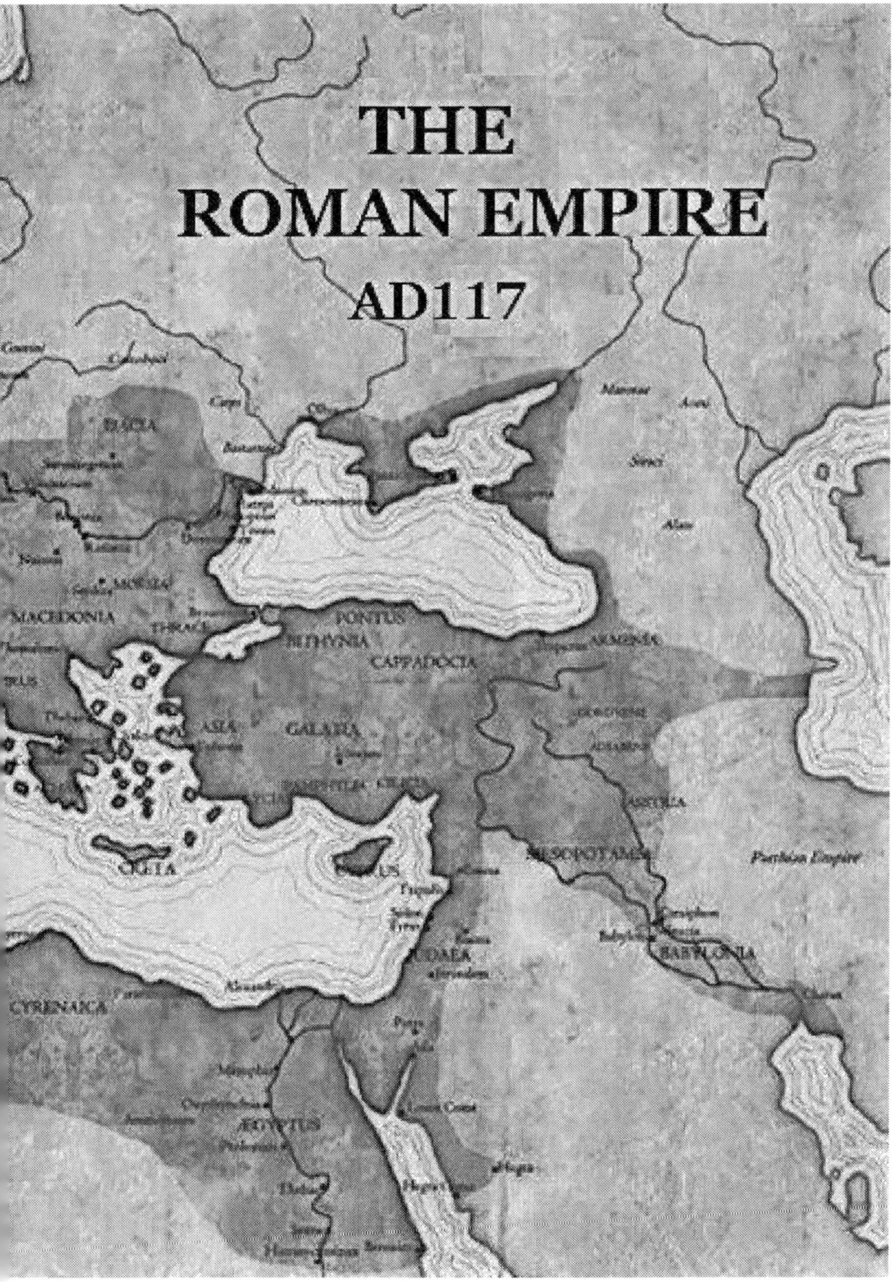

The Darker shades show extent of the Roman Empire in AD117 at its peak, approximately 60 years after Boudica's revolt.

Following the rebellion, for nearly 1,700 years Boudica and her revolt were largely forgotten. Memories of the revolt were often discouraged as insecure British rulers were not inclined to celebrate rebellious sentiment.

This all changed with the coming of the Victorian era and the expansion of the British Empire. In 1837, at the age of 18, Victoria became Queen of Great Britain and Ireland. Victoria, once enthroned, felt relatively secure as did the government of the day. With the Empire expanding rapidly, the Victorians drew inspiration from the Roman Empire's achievements whilst strangely at the same time celebrating Boudica's rebellion against it. Thus, Boudica's legend was revived by the establishment without fear and embellished at will.

Much of the knowledge of Boudica/Boadicea, even her existence and rebellion, has come from just two sources, Romans or those in the employ of the Romans, in other words the winning side. The first known account was written about 40 years after the rebellion and the second some 140 years later. The 'bible' of our knowledge of the revolt is taken from *Annals of Imperial Rome* written by the Roman writer Cornelius Tacitus. This covers the period from approximately AD14 to AD68. Yet, Michaels Grant's 1956 comprehensive translation of the work devotes only five pages to the revolt within a 400 page book.

There are no 'on the spot' eyewitness accounts or near contemporary British/English records of the rebellion whatsoever. All subsequent books written about Boudica/Boadicea rely heavily on the narratives of the two above Roman sources and are supplemented by some archaeological finds. Other tales of the revolt are speculative, informed or otherwise or simply fiction.

Another aspect to put the revolt into context is the size of the indigenous population of England which was tiny as compared with the present. The best guess, and it is no more than a guess, is that the population of England and Wales in AD60/61 was between half a million and a million. That's about one fiftieth of the current population count. Very little is known about Boudica personally. There is no detail of her early life or where she came from. She was simply described as the Queen of the East Anglian Iceni tribe and widow of the Iceni King Prasutagus.

She is said by the Greek/Roman author Cassius Dio (writing 140 years after the revolt) as being 'huge of frame with bright red hair which fell to her knees'. She is said to have 'worn a dress of many colours with a big gold chain and a brooch to hold her outer mantle (cape)'. Boudica had two daughters, yet the names or ages of the daughters are unknown. Boudica's age is also not revealed. It is assumed that at the time of the rebellion Boudica was in her early thirties.

Just to add to the confusion, in the 1970s the name Boadicea fell out of use and was replaced by Boudicca or Boudica. Using a single c or double c became optional. Throughout this book Boudica is the spelling used.

Please note this is not an academic reference book. My aim is, as best as possible, to try and separate the fact, as such, from fiction and what was plausible during the revolt. Throughout the book English town and city names have been used as opposed to the Latin ones. On page 11 the English and Latin versions are shown.

Unfortunately, it has not been easy to simplify the Roman or English tribal names, Boudica perhaps being the exception. Nearly all the Roman names and several of the English tribal kings, whether using first or surnames, end with ius, us, or nus.

Queen Boudica

Some are born great, some achieve greatness,
and some have greatness thrust upon them?
(*William Shakespeare*)
Malvolio with Olivia
ACT III SCENE IV
Twelfth Night

Part I

What We Know

What's in a Name?

Boadicea, Boudica, Boudicca, Bodicca, Budiga, Buddag, Bunduca, Voadicia, Voada, Θρίαμβος (Thríamvos) are just some of the names attributed to the title character of this book. The last name is a Greek version which means triumph. The other Latin, Celtic or Gaelic versions roughly mean 'Victory' or 'She brings victory'. With these descriptions, although the legend has it that she was wife to King Presutagus, even if she had not been a queen, Boudica would be a great name for a war leader. Assuming that Boudica was in her thirties at the time of the revolt, AD60/61, she would have been born around AD30. It must have been remarkable foresight on the part of her parents to call their child 'She brings victory' at least thirteen years before the Roman occupation began in AD43. Of course, the Iceni were continually fighting other British tribes off and on so the name may have been apt. Alternatively, in the absence of any contemporary evidence, the name Boudica (or Boadicea) could simply have been given to her by the Roman writers.

Continuing with the name though, over 1400 years after the revolt, in Scotland, King James IV made Hector Böece the first principal of the new Aberdeen University. In 1527, Böece published his *History of the Scottish People* in which he transposed the Boudican rebellion to Scotland renaming the heroine 'Voada'. Meanwhile in England, during the latter days of his reign, King Henry VII encouraged an Italian, Polydore Virgil, to write a history of England. Virgil was familiar with Boece's work and published his *Anglia Historia* in 1534. In it he used the name 'Voadicea'

In 1577, during the reign of Queen Elizabeth I, the author Raphael Holinshed also referred to Voadicea in his *Chronicles,* whilst the poet Edmund Spenser sympathetically referred to Bundaca in two of his poems and Boadicea was featured in a play by Ben Johnson. It is perhaps curious that Boadicea/Boudica was completely ignored by Shakespeare.

Shakespeare's only incursion into that period of early British history was *Cymbeline* a 'tragedy' vaguely based on Cunobelinus the King of the Catuvellauni. Although the real King Cunobelinus died before the Roman invasion of AD43, Shakespeare happily added Romans into the Cymbeline story.

The first biography of Boudica came in 1591 from an Italian living in England, Petruccio Ubaldini - *The Lives of the Noble Ladies of the Kingdom of England and Scotland*. In this work he suggests Boudica was in fact two women, Voadicea and Bunduica. Voadicea was described as honourable and noble, whereas Bunduica was savage and cruel.

In 1611, John Speed, in his *History of Great Britaine,* referred to Boudica, Voadica and Boduo. Later the story of Bonduca was told in a play by John Fletcher, performed by Shakespeare's *The King's Men* in 1613. The play was adapted several times over the next 100 years.

The writings about Boudica varied wildly in their portrayals. Some described her as the dominant figure whilst others had her as a subsidiary character. In the 1670s John Milton, the poet and author, was most uncomplimentary about the insurrection, describing the rebels as barbarians without foresight, confused, impotent and led by a wild distracted woman. Yet other poets had different opinions. At the time of the imminent loss of the American Colonies, the poet William Cowper, in 1782, published a glowing tribute to Boadicea in his *Boadicea an Ode*. Yet, despite whatever was written from the Tudor period onwards all authors drew inspiration from the chronicles of the two Roman authors or later works lifted from them.

As the 19th century dawned, the name Boadicea seems to have become established. It continued to be used into and throughout Victorian times without question and then into the 20th century until the 1960s without challenge - but that was about to change.

Sometime in the late 1960s or early 1970's, we can't be specific on the date, a group of scholars, led by the late Prof Kenneth Jackson, a

Celtic language specialist, confirmed that there had been a typo in one of translations in the Middle Ages from a manuscript by the Roman author Tacitus. Thus, Boadicea was to became Boudica spelt with one or two cs and this has been the accepted use ever since.

The name change led to confusion. As early as 1937, the author Lewis Spence who penned *Boadicea, Warrior Queen of the Britons* wrote 'Scholars would not have us say *Boadicea*, but *Boudica*.

WHAT'S in a NAME? **Boadicea**, Boudica, Boudicca, **Bodicca**, *Budiga*, **BUDDAG,** Bunduca, Voadicia, *Voada*, **Θρίαμβος (Thríamvos)** Boadicea, Boudica, Boudicca, **Bodicca**, *Budiga*, **BUDDAG,** Bunduca, Voadicia, *Voada*, **Θρίαμβος (Thríamvos)** Boadicea, Boudica, Boudicca, **Bodicca**, *Budiga*, **BUDDAG,** Bunduca, Voadicia, *Voada*, Θρίαμβος (Thríamvos) Boadicea, Boudica, Boudicca, **Bodicca**, *Budiga*, **BUDDAG,** Bunduca, Voadicia, *Voada*, Θρίαμβος (Thríamvos) Boadicea, Boudica, Boudicca, **Bodicca**, *Budiga*, **BUDDAG,** Bunduca, Voadicia, *Voada*, Θρίαμβος (Thríamvos)

Just over 30 years later, the late James Maurice Scott published a detailed account entitled, *BOADICEA, Queen of the Iceni who died in AD61 after leading her people against the Roman Invader*. In his preface he wrote: -

Scholars are now agreed that the person with whom this book is concerned should be named Boudicca or perhaps Boudica being a derivation from the Welsh buddug or more ancient buddig – both meaning victory. Despite the scholarly advice Scott (and also Spence) stuck with *Boadicea*. Scott summed up and commented dryly, *with **Boadicea** as the title, some may be critical, but at least everyone will know what the book is about!* That was back in 1969. Over the following 50 years the scholarly advice was heeded and today *Boudica* spelt with a single c or a double c is generally accepted.

Before the Romans

Over the centuries the seas around the British Isles didn't deter settlers arriving. As a rule, once settled, they preferred to live in the upper elevation of river valleys and lowland plains free from flooding with good drainage, where they could fish, grow crops, and graze animals. Other than the most rudimentary, there were no flood defences. Much of England was forested which was another constraint on the inhabitants.

Before the Romans – on the lookout for incursions by hostile tribes

They tended to live outside thickly wooded areas until they developed tools enabling them to cut down heavy oak or ash trees to make clearings. Consequently, the 'habitable' areas, even for the very low population of the British Isles, were at times fiercely fought over. This may have accounted for the warlike nature of some of the tribes. Before the Romans colonisation, the population of the British Isles was divided into various tribes with unique identities. In no sense was the British Isles a unified nation. In England, of Celtic origin, the Iceni lived in East Anglia and the Trinovantes had settled around Colchester and mid Essex. Other Celtic tribes lived in the north of England and Wales. Approximately 25 years before Caesar's first incursions into Britain the Belgae began to arrive in England. They were a confederation of tribes living in what is today Belgium, Northern France and parts of western Germany.

One branch of the Belgae was the Catuvellauni who established a fortified capital at Wheathampstead north of St Albans. The tribe quickly spread east, frequently fighting with the Trinovantes. Another Belgic tribe, the Atrebates, also displaced from France, settled in Silchester in Berkshire and ruthlessly drove out other tribes living in the locality.

Despite their differences with Rome, the Belgae maintained strong commercial and cultural links with the Roman Empire. These links grew steadily between Julius Caesar's first incursion in 55BC and the full invasion of Emperor Claudius nearly 100 years later.

If nothing else the arrival of the Romans in force in AD43 heralded the beginning of a cessation of the British tribal infighting and the seeds of *Pax Romana*.

Setting the Scene - Julius Caesar

Veni, vidi, vici

'I Came; I Saw; I Conquered.

The Roman Republic which later became the Roman Empire came into existence around 500 BC and lasted for nearly 1000 years. It went through several phases of expansion reaching its peak around AD117 (see map pages 18/19).

Some 200 years before Julius Caesar's first foray into Britannia, a Greek sea captain, Pythias, sailed out of the Mediterranean into the stormy north Atlantic. He made landfall in Cornwall and recorded native craftsmen mining and then smelting tin which they traded with merchants from the continent. Pythias continued his voyage circumnavigating the British Isles and recording a land of many natural resources. His report was reinforced by stories from cross channel traders and merchants. For two centuries the Romans had viewed Britain as land of mystery, a land where there were many rulers who often fought each other using horse drawn chariots. As reports came back to Rome from Pythias and cross channel traders the view of Britain changed. The Romans and Caesar began to realise that this mysterious island could be a land of riches.

Julius Caesar had been busy fighting in the Gallic Wars. With military success in his French campaigns, he turned his attention to the British Isles. In 55BC he assembled a fleet of 70 ships to cross the channel with two legions of Roman soldiers, about 10,000 men. They landed near Deal in Kent.

The expedition did not go quite according to plan. The supply ships were stalled by storm force winds in the channel. Although the Romans secured the beachhead and easily swept aside any opposition, Caesar judged his position weak and withdrew back to France. There were no military gains of any significance to report, and the operation could be considered as no more than a reconnaissance mission, valuable, nevertheless.

However, Caesar considered that this new land was ripe for plucking as there were deposits of gold, silver and tin to be had. The animal hides were first class, clever hunting dogs were bred and there was a goodly supply of healthy slaves for the taking.

Although another invasion was a great risk personally, Julius Caesar was ambitious. He believed that by adding Britain, even in a limited way, to Roman possessions, such a move would enhance his prestige immensely.

Julius Caesar landed near here LV BC, Sculpture, Walmer Beach Kent

A year later, in 54BC, Caesar returned. This time he mustered 28,000 men (five legions and auxiliaries) and 2000 cavalry. Again the Romans landed in Kent this time near Pegwell Bay. As before, initial resistance from the assorted British tribes was easily swept aside but increased the further inland they marched. Catuvellauni lands stretched from Hertfordshire across the Thames to Surrey. The tribe was led by

Cassivellaunus, an aggressively expansionist leader. His tribe was also at war with their neighbours, among them the Trinovantes of Essex.

Following the landings, the legions marched on as far as St Albans despite constant harassment from the Catuvellauni. At St Albans, Caesar, who had gained the allegiance of the Essex based Trinovantes, was able to attack the Catuvellauni and destroy their stronghold. Although he was never captured, this decisive victory resulted in Cassivellaunus, along with many other tribal leaders, suing for peace.

With southeast Britain subdued, Caesar considered his expedition as a mission accomplished. Caesar returned to France after what he considered to be a brilliant campaign and contemplated another invasion the following year.

Caesar never returned as a revolt in France consumed all of his attention. Then fatally, infighting in Rome led to Caesar's assassination on March 15th 44BC, just 10 years after his triumph across the channel. Thereafter there was no Roman military presence in Britain for nearly 100 years.

Nevertheless, the desire in Rome to add the British Isles and all its riches to the Roman fold lived on. The death of Caesar ushered in Augustus, the first Emperor. Augustus was followed by Tiberius. Beset by difficulties within the existing Empire neither Augustus nor Tiberius personally showed any interest in the British Isles. However, the next Emperor, Caligula, described as both mad and tyrannical, was keen on invading Britannia.

Meanwhile in Britannia, Cunobelinus the new king of the Catuvellauni, the tribe centred around modern day St. Albans, once again invaded the territory of the Trinovantes in Essex. Colchester became the new Catuvellauni capital and coinage was even minted there. Cunobelinus ruled the joint Catuvellaunian and Trinovantian kingdom from Colchester. He had two sons, Togodumnus and Caratacus. A third or perhaps a son-in-law, Adminius, from Canterbury in Kent, ruled an area around the south coast of England. These lands were inhabited by the Cantiaci and Atrebates tribes.

In AD39 King Cunobelinus was taken ill which led to a family falling out. Togodumnus and Caratacus assumed power and forced Adminius into exile in Gaul. Cunobelinus died in AD42. Togodumnus succeeded to the throne and authorised Caratacus to begin campaigning against the Atrebates tribe.

Meanwhile the exiled Adminius, joined by several nobles from the Atrebates, had made his way to Rome to seek support from Emperor Caligula for a Roman invasion of Britain and therefore to relieve the siege of Atrebates lands by Caratacus.

After meeting Adminius, Caligula became enthusiastic about an invasion. He put together an invasion force on the French channel coast but the fleet never sailed. The reasons for this are unclear although with a madman in charge it is speculated the legions refused to embark on what they considered a very risky adventure. In response Caligula ordered his soldiers to attack the waves and gather seashells and claim the shells as the spoils of victory.

After no more than staring across the channel, Caligula returned to Rome where he was murdered by the guard. In January AD41, his uncle Claudius became the new Emperor. Despite Caligula's abortive invasion attempt, the British Isles were still very much on the Roman 'wish list'. Although there were no Roman forces in Britain, over the decades since Julius Ceasar's invasions friendly links with the Trinovantes, the Atrebates and the Cantiaci continued, the latter two tribes based in Hampshire, Sussex, and Kent. During their absence the Romans had also been gathering intelligence on the less friendly tribes. Claudius then saw an opportunity to invade in AD43 when the Atrebates tribe was threatened once more by the Catuvellauni.

An important factor as well in Roman minds was that continued conflict between the various British tribes threatened to disrupt the already lucrative trade with Rome.

The Romans are back

The new emperor Claudius planned the invasion carefully. Not only were 40,000 troops made ready but the all the logistics of a permanent occupation were set in place after the ground had been secured.

The Romans also drew up several diversions and decoys but on the day they were not needed as the landing on the Kent coast went unopposed.

Once the British realised the Romans were ashore, their forces regrouped. However, as was to show repeatedly in fighting the Romans, despite individual bravery, enthusiasm, and superior numbers, the Britons were no match for a well-trained disciplined opponent.

Even the much vaunted British war chariots gave the Britons no advantage. Although chariot drivers were highly skilled, they could make no headway against a deep Roman shield wall. The Romans soon realised that if they killed the horses, the chariots became useless leaving their drivers and passengers stranded where they could easily be picked off.

After the unopposed landing, the Romans marched north-west. The two sides clashed at the river Medway. During a two-day battle the Romans prevailed again. Togodumnus was killed but Caratacus escaped and fled west. So far, the Roman campaign had been ruthlessly efficient and swift. With the Trinovantes on side no serious opposition could be expected on their next objective which was Colchester the Catuvellauni/Trinovantes capital.

The Romans crossed the river Thames then halted in Essex. Up to this point Emperor Claudius had not been present in the campaign. It was his wish to lead the final push on Colchester. Word was sent to him back in Rome of the invasion's progress. Claudius arrived with his Imperial suite in the late summer. He allegedly brought with him a force of war elephants, apparently needed to finish off the battle, but more likely they were just for show as victory was assured.

With little or no opposition across Essex, Claudius entered Colchester. Whether he rode in atop one of his war elephants is not recorded. He immediately set to work establishing a viable Roman presence on the British Isles. As far as he was concerned the Romans were here to stay this time. One of the first actions Claudius took was to make a series of treaties with the English tribes to bring about the Roman vision of *Pax Romana*.

Claudius returned to Rome. Nine years later the *Arch of Claudius* celebrating his achievements was dedicated in Rome. This recorded 'eleven kings of the Britons submitted' although the kings are not named.

Aulus Plautius, the military commander and now the Governor of the newly conquered land, was left in charge to implement the Emperor's wishes. The first need was to make the province secure and one of his subordinates, Vespasian, (who 16 years later became Roman Emperor himself) was ordered to sweep westwards to root out any lingering opposition.

Plautius then made Colchester his base, which sowed the first seeds of the trouble to come later from Boudica. Making Colchester a Roman town meant taking land from the local Trinovantes who up to that point had been Roman allies. With the whole of South-Eastern England considered secure, Aulus Plautius returned to Rome in AD 47. In turn, in the autumn, he was replaced by Ostorious Scapula. Colchester's name was changed too. Camulodunum, derived from the Celtic war god Camulos, was renamed the Colonia Claudia Victricensis (the colony of Claudius the Victorious) and was designated as a place for retired to soldiers to live.

Almost as soon as Scapula took up his post Caratacus, the surviving son of Cunobelinus, who escaped the original Roman onslaught at the battle on the river Medway, chose his moment to strike. Since his escape four years earlier Caratacus had been rallying his supporters and cultivating the local tribe, the Silures, with anti-

Roman sentiment. The arrival of a new Governor and the Roman legions hunkering down in their winter quarters seemed an ideal time to strike.

From bases in Wales, Caratacus crossed the River Severn and overran several frontier forts before striking deep into Roman occupied England and shattering the *Pax Romana*. Scapula decided he couldn't wait to consult the emperor on what action to take so decided to hunt Caratacus down and drive the rebels back into Wales.

The legions were roused from their winter quarters and despatched on a many pronged advance into the Welsh heartlands. The Roman governor was taking a great gamble. By attacking Wales he had severely depleted his forces in East Anglia. Whilst that area was generally secure any word of rebellion in other parts of the province could have unforeseen consequences.

All the while Colchester, the new capital, was growing. As mentioned it had been designated as a home or *colonia* for 'old' soldiers.

These men had been retired from active frontline service but were by no means incapable of fighting in an emergency or enforcing the local law in their own rough way. The atmosphere was not helped by the veterans' contemptuous attitude to the natives which was storing up problems for the future. As the numbers of 'retired soldiers' grew ever more numerous, it meant more and more land was appropriated from the existing local owners.

Nevertheless, for Governor Scapula, the creation of the new *Colonia* for veterans enabled local garrison troops to be released for the assault on Wales. Scapula took another gamble in that he ordered that the eastern tribes be disarmed. This caused a great deal of resentment. Many of the weapons and armour were family heirlooms passed down through the generations and were not readily handed over. Additionally confiscating weapons by its very nature usually involved an aggressive search into what were essentially private homes.

Caratacus having been freed by Emperor Claudius spent the rest of his life in Rome in exile with his family.

Once Scapula had what he considered sufficient force at his disposal he headed for Wales. Despite the onset of winter, the campaign was relatively short. At the battle of Caer Caradoc on the English/ Welsh border, in today's English county of Shropshire, Caratacus was surrounded and, after hard days fighting, the Romans were victorious, although somehow Caratacus managed to evade capture. He crossed the river Mersey into the tribal land of the Brigantes but there his luck ran out.

Queen Cartimandua of the Brigantes with whom Caratacus sought sanctuary was pro-Roman (unlike her husband). The unfortunate Caratacus was chained and handed over to the occupiers. He was taken to Rome and paraded on the streets and exhibited as part of Claudius's great triumph over the British tribes. Later Caratacus was brought before Emperor Claudius himself where it is said he made a moving speech which so impressed the Emperor that he and his family were granted a pardon and permitted to live in exile in Italy peacefully for the rest of their lives.

For Scapula, the Roman governor, the capture of Caratacus had not solved the 'Welsh' difficulty. Raids continued from Wales. Whatever they tried the Romans seemed unable to track down this elusive enemy. Consequently, Scapula's health broke and he died.

The new Governor appointed by Rome in AD52 was Didius Gallus, a former senator and military commander. Gallus was described as unenterprising and dull, and he remained in post for six years. During his tenure the situation in Britain remained much the same. Although there were constant raids by disgruntled rebels from Wales, the situation was contained overall and East Anglia and Southern England remained calm. Although nothing much changed in Roman ruled Britannia there were dramatic upheavals in Rome. The Emperor Claudius died after being poisoned. He was replaced by the seventeen-year-old Lucius Domitius Ahenobarbus, more commonly called Nero.

For the first few years of his reign, Nero was cautious in his actions and followed the advice of his councillors. In respect of the British Isles, although the province was deemed rich, as yet it hadn't made a return for the enormous investment put in.

Britannia was also far from Rome at the western edge of the empire, separated by sea from the mainland, the weather in Roman eyes was awful and frontier garrison costs simply too expensive to keep. Nero's advisors even suggested withdrawing and writing the whole province off as uneconomic.

Five years into his reign Nero felt strong enough to make his own decisions. He decided that, despite the risks, the nettle of Britain must be grasped and be made to pay its way. This meant the Welsh question had to be dealt with for once and for all.

A new governor for the British Isles was appointed, Quintus Veranius, a distinguished general who had a reputation of initiative and drive. Veranius boasted to Nero that he would conquer the whole of the British Isles within two years. Yet within a year the general had died, apparently due to the British climate.

The New Governor

Suetonius Paulinus

The unexpected death of Quintus Veranius created an unplanned hiatus in the Roman governorship of Britain and finding a suitable candidate for the post was a time-consuming process exacerbated by the distances involved. Just notifying Rome of the death could take four to five weeks. Then a successor had to be agreed by the Roman Senate. To qualify, the new Governor had to be from the military with a proven track record and just as important politically acceptable to the authorities in Rome. Even then, when the choice had been made, the candidate had to be recalled from anywhere in the far flung Roman Empire. That process could take another two months.

The successor chosen, Suetonius Paulinus, was described as a man of action experienced in mountain warfare having been the first Roman to cross the Atlas Mountains in North Africa and lead his force to effectively suppress a revolt in Mauretania.

Boudica's Nemesis
Suetonius Paulinus

However, there was more delay before Paulinus could take up his new post. He had to be briefed by the numerous departments of state on the situation in Britannia so far as it was understood. Also his headquarters staff needed to be appointed, both military and clerical. Joining Paulinus on the military side was a young staff officer, 18-year-old Julius Agricola.

Suetonius Paulinus arrived in Britain in the autumn of AD58. His primary task was to deal with the Welsh question. Following the death of the previous governor Veranius, his deputy and second in command, the Procurator, Decianus Catus, had acted as Governor. The Procurator's usual responsibility was to oversee the civil administration and supervise all matters connected with revenue especially tax gathering. Catus seemed to have relished the position of acting governor as it had given him additional financial powers to extract even more money from the 'natives'. As for general security, whilst Catus was in charge the individual legion commanders did their best to maintain law and order and keep the Welsh marauders at bay. In general *Pax Romana* was maintained.

However, the underwhelming rule of the previous two Governors, Gallus and Veranius, the absence of a governor after Veranius's death and leaving Catus in charge was stoking up ever more resentment. In his desire to keep the British tribes quiet Catus had enabled or perhaps encouraged money lenders (by no means all reputable) to give generous loans and other favours to the client tribal kings and their nobility.

When the new Governor Suetonius Paulinus eventually arrived, he was a man in a hurry. There was a job to be done. The Procurator Catus presumably assured Paulinus that everything was under control in East Anglia and that he was more than capable of dealing with any local difficulties. Colchester, the de-facto capital of the British Isles, was being rapidly built up. The showpiece Temple of Claudius (which originally stood on the site that is now Colchester castle) had just been completed as had a senate house and even the trappings of a theatre were being built.

Colchester lay in the land of the Trinovantes, the tribe that had meekly accepted subjugation and had cooperated in turning Colchester into a showpiece Roman town as part of the integration process. Whatever doubts had been expressed in Rome as to the future of the British colony, the Romans in Colchester were determined to stay.

Yet the construction and upkeep of fine buildings costs money. The Romans had no intention of paying for all the costs themselves. Taxes were increased for the wealthier Trinovantes. Other locals were rounded up as slave labour on the construction projects. All the while the swelling numbers of legionary veterans living in Colchester required more and more living space. They grabbed more land at will and conscripted the former owners to work for them.

These actions may have been outside the law, but the Governor, through Catus, chose to ignore them no matter how flagrant the breeches were. Whatever happened the veterans could be relied upon to quell any resistance.

As Suetonius Paulinus set off for Wales, all seemed in order. The towns of Colchester (Camulodunum), the defacto capital, London (Londinum), a growing merchant city, and further to the north St Albans (Verulamium) in the heart of the conquered Catuvellauni territory formed a supposedly secure triangle. The Romans were surrounded by the lands of client kings in whose interest it was to keep their own people in line. Yet, this was only a temporary arrangement. The client kingdoms would be taken over one by one and absorbed into the Roman fold as soon as the Romans deemed the time was right.

This was the Roman way and had been the basis of Claudius's settlement when he had marched into Colchester back in AD43. It is now pertinent to mention King Prasutagus of the Iceni.

King Prasutagus
and the Iceni

The Iceni tribe occupied the territory that encompasses much of present-day Norfolk and Suffolk. According to the Roman historians, and supported by more recent archaeological finds, the Iceni were a wealthy people with their own coinage. However, none of the first century coins since found can be linked to Prasutagus or Boudica. Julius Caesar commented also that the Iceni were skilled horsemen and women.

Unfortunately, there is nothing to show where the Iceni centre of power lay or where Prasutagus, Boudica and their family lived. In fact, it is only the Roman writers Tacitus and Cassius Dio's written records that tell of their actual existence and their names.

In AD43 when Emperor Claudius first arrived in Colchester, it is presumed the Iceni were one of the eleven tribal kingdoms that submitted to Rome. It is not known whether King Prasutagus was party to the agreement and thereafter a client king of Rome but it was the first indication of any political organisation on the part of the Iceni. Nevertheless, the agreement gained the Iceni Roman protection, and they were generally left free to govern themselves.

Until the arrival of the Romans, the Iceni suffered regular incursions from neighbouring tribes and as a matter of course they retaliated. The Roman occupation was designed to ensure boundaries were set and peace between the tribes prevailed – the *Pax Romana*.

For four years the Iceni/Roman agreement held until the Roman Governor Scapula began his programme of disarmament as mentioned on page 35. The Iceni revolted, not against the Romans in general but against the intrusive measures of the disarmament process. The revolt was quickly supressed and from that time King Prasutagus was known to be king of the Iceni. When he became King though remains a matter of speculation.

The archaeologist and academic Miranda Aldhouse-Green speculated that after the revolt about arms confiscation, Prasutagus was conveniently elevated by the Romans to be the King of the Iceni. He was seen as being suitably compliant in keeping the peace and sticking to the terms of dividing his kingdom on his death.

King Prasutagus died in AD59 without a male heir. According to the settlement agreed with Rome sixteeen years earlier, on his death his lands and private wealth would be divided equally between his two daughters and the Romans. It is interesting to note that Boudica, the king's wife was not named as a beneficiary of his will. Aldhouse-Green notes the significance of this omission in the king's will as evidence of Queen Boudica's distrust and hostility towards Rome even before the shocking events that came to pass that are described later. King Prasutagus, perhaps naively, hoped his daughters would follow his policy of cooperation and the Iceni would continue to rely on the Romans to protect them from the ravages of other English tribes.

The Roman Campaign in Wales

Suetonius Paulinus, on taking command, was fortunate in that his new province had reasonably good communications from the south to the north-west. Since the Romans arrival in force 15 years earlier a road building programme had been mapped out and construction started. Like Roman roads in other parts of the Empire such roads were solidly built for all weather, fit for all types of traffic and generally in straight lines through the countryside. Good roads enabled messages to be sent quickly. Even Roman legions could march fully equipped across the country in little over a week, although the heavy baggage trains would take longer.

Despite the professionalism and first-class training of the Roman soldiers, Wales presented a real challenge. The land was mountainous and the Roman roads did not extend there. They also lacked detailed knowledge of the enemy or the land they were destined to fight in and had few spies to call on for local intelligence.

The Romans had to contend with three Welsh tribes, all implacably hostile. The Silures, in the south-east above the Bristol channel and Severn estuary, the Ordovices, covering most of the mountainous centre of Wales as far as Snowdonia, and the Degeangli who lived in Flintshire bordering the River Dee estuary. The Silures had given full support to Caratacus in his attacks on the Romans. Even after Caratacus was taken prisoner the Silures continued with hit and run raids despite the best efforts of previous governors to persuade them otherwise.

Although Suetonius Paulinus had command of two full legions plus auxiliaries, he knew he had no easy task. The Isle of Anglesey in the top north-east corner of Wales was considered the ultimate objective. Anglesey was the Welsh granary and storehouse and the last resort shelter for dissidents. Also the Druids, the mysterious prophets and mystics, had a strong presence in Anglesey and used every opportunity to stir up resentment against the Romans.

Paulinus decided on a two-pronged assault. Starting in Wroxeter one legion would cross the river Severn south-east of Shrewsbury and march west though the mountains and strike north along the coastal plain via Porthmadog, (Portmadoc) towards what is now Bangor. The second legion departed from Chester and moved north and west around the Flintshire coast to complete a pincer movement. This plan would contain any insurgents in the mountains and keep them away from their store house on Anglesey.

Anglesey is separated from the mainland by the Menai Straits which is roughly 300 metres wide at its narrowest point. The Governor called up the Roman fleet and added several newly built flat-bottomed boats to carry the infantry. By the spring of AD60 the Roman expeditionary force was assembled on the shore facing Anglesey. So far the campaign had lasted nearly two years but the end was in sight.

The Menai Straits

On Anglesey, facing the Romans, was the remaining hard core of British resistance massed on the shore. They were egged on by the Druid priests shouting prayers and curses and fanatical women dressed in black running about and screaming. Yet the resistance did not have a single military strategist among them.

For the Romans the sight of the Druids was unnerving, but fanaticism could not provide effective resistance. Despite some initial doubts the Romans easily crossed the Menai Straits and once their war machine was unleashed the defenders were cut down or trampled to death by the advancing cavalry.

For Suetonius Paulinus, now well past his middle age, the campaign in Wales had been a triumph. The most westerly part of the British Isles was now in Roman hands. However, as he savoured his victory, word came – rebellion had broken out in East Anglia 300 miles away.

The Menai Bridge connecting the mainland to Anglesey (Mons) where 2000 years ago Paulinus received word of the Boudica's uprising

The Coming Storm

For Suetonius Paulinus the campaign in Wales had always been a risky strategy. He had stripped out more than half of the Roman forces serving in Britain. This had left the country exposed to hostile incursions from the north or west or local insurrections in East Anglia. The Welsh campaign took nearly two years and, although a military success, the Roman legions leading the fight were depleted in numbers and the legionnaires exhausted.

Although presumably sad for the Iceni and the king's family, the death of Prasutagus couldn't have come at a worse time for Paulinus. In his absence, Procurator Catus Decianus had been left in charge. He was fully aware of the division of spoils on Prasutagus's death and he must have viewed this as an opportunity to turn the situation to his advantage.

During the Roman occupation the Iceni had been free from incursions by other English tribes. Iceni royalty and close supporters had prospered under Roman rule. Many Iceni nobles had taken advantage of long-term loans offered by 'money lenders' or their agents approved by the Procurator. It is reported that Seneca, one of Emperor Nero's former tutors, had vast sums of money tied up in private loans in Britain.

The belief in the superiority of Romans was personified in Catus. He had no regard for tribal feelings. The tribes were reliant on Roman protection from attacks by one another and *Pax Romana* was the cornerstone of keeping the peace. The local tribes were simply considered as too timid, too stupid, or both to revolt against their new masters.

Despite the absence of Suetonius Paulinus with most of the army, there was still a full legion, the IX, billeted in Lincoln that could be called upon to help if needed. There was a good road from there to the south and several fortified compounds throughout East-Anglia.

Catus' contempt for the locals increasingly led to much of their land being expropriated for the 'veterans' in Colchester. Even landowners allowed to remain on their farms were expected to provide grain and other foodstuffs at prices determined by the Romans. Many of those evicted or dispossessed had to work as slaves for new masters. Catus saw the Trinovantes as weak; the more they submitted, the more they could be abused.

The death of King Prasutagus gave Procurator Catus Decianus, the opportunity to turn his attention to the Iceni. Meetings with leaders were swiftly arranged in order claim the land and wealth - the fifty percent agreed (see page 42). A full tax assessment (or census) that had begun under the previous Governor, Quintus Veranius, was speeded up. For the Iceni this stirred memories of the intrusive disarmament process carried out some years before which added to the general air of resentment.

Catus' next move was to demand the return of money loaned to elite Britons during the reign of Emperor Claudius. Seneca, suddenly doubtful of his investment, demanded the return of all the money he had loaned (at high interest). Other loans were called in to which fifteen years of unpaid interest was added. Where the loans could not be repaid immediately, land and property was simply seized. In the meantime, in and around Colchester the veterans continued with the expropriation of lands, evicting or enslaving the inhabitants.

The ultimate violation though was about to happen. It is not known who on the Roman side took part, or where it happened, and it seems Decianus was not present. A Roman cohort arrived unannounced at the Iceni Royal Palace. It immediately became clear that this was not a visit to express sympathy for the deceased king or condolences to the widow. Nor was it a business meeting to sort the details of the agreed settlement. There had been a change of plan. The Romans who arrived demanded everything not just the fifty percent. The Iceni kingdom was to be annexed in full.

The Roman author Tacitus described Catus as 'rapacious', and largely to blame for provoking the rebellion of Boudica. Cassius Dio said of Catus he was 'graceless, cruel, and avaricious'.

The Final Straw

As mentioned in the introduction little is known of the Queen. We may assume the King, Queen and their daughters were a happy family and well loved by their people. Boudica, driving her chariot at speed, her long red hair streaming in the wind with her two girls by her side, happy, holding on tightly and laughing as the chariot bumped along the road is an image conjured up by writers and artists over the years. It is also perhaps fair to assume that Queen Boudica was aware of her husband's will and the settlement terms agreed with Rome; that her daughters would inherit and the result would be the Iceni nobility would be left in peace much as before.

When Catus's men arrived at the Royal Palace, Boudica must have sensed something was amiss. There were no pleasantries. The writer Tacitus describes *the men from Colchester as having nothing exempted from their avarice and nothing from their lust.* The Romans just barged in. When the demands for everything were presented, there must have been an explosion. It is assumed Boudica would not have taken the intrusion quietly.

As far as these Roman intruders were concerned the Iceni were an inferior race and barbarians to boot. Resistance shown, especially from women, was treated with utter contempt. As all this happened Boudica was no doubt and understandably in a rage. Consequently, she was seized, bound and flogged, then, shockingly, both her daughters were raped in full view of their mother. Having delivered the procurator's message, the Romans departed, taking as much loot from the palace as they could carry.

The rebellion of Boudica was noted for its atrocious cruelties. A mother who has been humiliated, tied, and beaten and in all probability seen her daughters raped in front of her would unsurprising be filled with rage. A desire to kill could not have been far from her mind. The Romans had originally brought a degree of stability to the land. The laws were clear, but where were the laws now as the Iceni felt the full force of Roman brutality? Their homes were being looted and their leaders humiliated. The actions directed by Catus had unleashed an uncontrollable tide of hatred.

Following the palace outrage there was no immediate outburst from the Iceni people. Boudica possessed qualities she may not have known she had. She found, despite the personal outrages she suffered, she could control not only herself, but the Iceni people who were not known for their discipline.

A line from William Shakespeare's play *Twelfth Night* written 1500 years after the Boudican revolt reads: -

Some are born great, some achieve greatness, and some have greatness thrust upon them.

The words could well have applied to Boudica. Realising her power, she set to work like a seasoned general. It is also perhaps surprising that we learn again of this from the Roman chroniclers.

In the spring of AD60 or 61 Boudica organised a series of clandestine meetings, not only of the Iceni but with representatives of the Trinovantes and perhaps even of the Catuvellauni too. The meetings or conferences were all held on Iceni land where one delegate after another told of how they and their people had been plundered and abused by their Roman overlords. The meetings were arranged with extraordinary skill. Secrecy was paramount. Although the Romans had a widespread network of spies and retainers, they learned nothing of the meetings.

However, if word had actually reached Catus about the meetings he in all probability would have dismissed them with contempt. In his view the natives were totally unable to organise anything together.

History had shown that the British tribes were notoriously individualistic and unruly, so it is a tribute to Boudica's remarkable organisational ability and force of personality that she was able to get the tribes to work together. With a consensus agreed, weapons and stores were collected. The fighters were assembled and a campaign strategy finalised. How this was done under the noses of the Romans without any of the details leaking remains a mystery it itself.

Colchester was selected as their first target. This after all was the Roman capital, the heart of the beast, and symbolised by the monstrous Temple of Claudius. Above all Colchester was where the hated veterans were based, the ones responsible for much of the abuse and outrage.

Fooling the Roman spies, Boudica gathered an army of some 100,000. She is reported by the writer Cassius Dio to have addressed them from her royal chariot, her eyes blazing, with her bright red hair blowing in the wind. Her voice was passionate but terrifying in its fury and soon Boudica had worked her army into a frenzy. Colchester was about to feel the full might of an avenging army lusting for blood.

Blood and Fire

The timeline now is blurred. April or May of AD61 is the best guess as to the beginning of the so-called fighting season. Whilst three hundred miles to the north-west of Colchester, Governor Paulinus' legions were making their final assault on Anglesey, Boudica's coalition forces were snaking through the forests of Norfolk, Suffolk and into Essex towards the unguarded Colchester.

Boudica's hordes swept past the assorted outlying Roman Garrison forts leaving them surrounded and the soldiers trapped. They would be dealt with later. The secret was out. The rebels' direction and target were now obvious. Some Roman messengers escaped the noose and news of the rebellion soon reached the IX Legion in Lincoln, commanded by Petilius Cerialis. Governor Paulinus, camped out facing Anglesey, received word shortly after.

Yet as Boudica closed in on Colchester the inhabitants and veteran soldiers were overcome by a collective paralysis. An air of gloom hung over the colony. The statue of victory erected to celebrate the Romans' arrival, which stood proudly in front of the Temple of Claudius, mysteriously toppled over. It lay on the ground with its goddess' face pressed earthwards as if to show she had yielded to the enemies of Rome. Around the town groups of women ran screaming of impending doom and the council chamber and even the theatre were plagued by fearful howling. Then news came of a vision seen by sailors in the mouth of the river Thames showing the colony in ruins and the sea purple with blood.

There was talk of digging defensive ditches and throwing up barriers, but nothing was done. No effort was made to move the vulnerable, the sick or women and children to safety. There was a feeling the colony was cursed and deserved the fate to be visited upon it. An urgent plea for help was sent to Procurator Catus in London. Accordingly, two hundred men were sent as reinforcements.

Intoxicated with hatred, Boudica's tribal coalition fell upon Colchester sweeping all before them. No quarter was given and no prisoners taken. All was to be burned to cleanse the land of the oppressors. The destruction was methodical and calculating. The survivors of the first onslaught and their families retreated into the Temple of Claudius for sanctuary. They held out for two days but their sanctuary became a crematorium. Any who escaped the flames were then killed in the most sadistic and brutal way imaginable. It is not known what happened to the reinforcements sent by Catus from London. Whether they got to Colchester or perished in the destruction is a mystery.

Boudica may have wanted to stop or at least pause at that point but it was not possible. She had her own local spies and word came that the IX legion was on route from Lincoln.

There, 150 miles distant, Petilius Cerialis, on hearing of the attack, rallied the IX legion and marched south. There was a goodish road network that linked Lincoln to Colchester. It was possible the lightly equipped soldiers could march up to 30 miles a day, although the supply train following them would be much slower. Cerialis supposed that even if he couldn't save Colchester, he could still get there in a few days and then inflict severe damage on Boudica and her rabble of barbarians.

Boudica had other ideas. Somewhere along Ermine Street, which roughly followed today's A1, Great North Road, Ceralis' column was ambushed by the rebels. The legion's infantry, some 2000 men, was cut down. Petilius Cerialis was lucky to escape with his life and retreated to Lincoln with his cavalry. Unfortunately, none of the Roman writers indicate where this ambush took place. There has been speculation that the ambush took place somewhere near Cambridge although no evidence has been found to support this.

The author Tacitus summed up the ambush on the 9th legion in just a few lines.

The victorious enemy met Petilius Cerialis, commander of the ninth legion, as he was coming to the rescue, routed his troops, and destroyed all his infantry. Ceralias escaped with some cavalry into the camp, and was saved by its fortifications. The Annals, Book XIV (32).

We do not know if Boudica led this ambush. However, whether she did or did not, it showed superb battlefield tactics on the part of the rebels. More worryingly for the Romans, the tribal forces had succeeded in destroying a regular army unit rather than just a defenceless town.

It didn't take long for the news of this new disaster to reach the Governor in Wales. For Suetonius Paulinus what had seemed a small insurrection to begin with was turning into a catastrophe of epic proportions.

Planning for the worst

Governor Paulinus, camped on the shores of Anglesey, knew he had to act quickly. He couldn't afford to bask in the glory of an achievement that had eluded his predecessors - capturing Anglesey and destroying the Druid stronghold. Paulinus was a military man through and through and a skilled tactician. He was little interested in the niceties of the law and civil administration. He had no time for the bureaucracy attached to them. He was not a young man, well into middle age, he planned carefully but at the same time he was willing to take risks. He was hard, efficient, and expected loyalty and discipline from those he commanded. His reputation would stand or fall on how the military situation on the British Isles was resolved.

Looking at the map the Governor's options seemed limited. Colchester had fallen. The IX Legion had been routed. By all accounts his enemy had an army numbering over 100,000 and growing. London and St Albans appeared to be the next targets of the rebel hordes. On the other hand, the soldiers he had led into Wales for two campaigning seasons were tired and reduced by attrition.

Furthermore, even if his legions were at peak strength and condition they could only withdraw slowly. Although most of the enemy in Anglesey had been wiped out, there were still plenty of rebels, masters of deadly surprise, hiding out in the mountains.

Paulinius calculated that if he could get to London before Boudica, there was a chance of saving the city. Speed was critical. He rounded up his small force of cavalry and set off. The infantry were ordered to follow.

Messengers were sent ahead to Gloucester, where the II Legion was stationed, with orders for them to join the Governor at a point where the Roman Fosse Way intersected with Watling Street at High Cross (Venonis). This was on today's A5 approximately half way between Rugby and Leicester. Sadly, none of this can be confirmed but in the end it was all irrelevant as the II Legion never arrived at High Cross.

A subordinate, Poenius Postumas, was in command and for reasons also unknown gave no order for the II Legion to move. Postumas later committed suicide. If the II Legion had joined the cavalry the Governor would have had a more balanced force to defend London. Yet it would still be tiny compared to Boudica's numbers.

Nevertheless, the absence of reinforcements didn't deter Paulinus. He galloped on making about 50 miles a day. Fortunately for Paulinus, the rebel's ambush of the IX Legion had enabled the Governor to reach London before Boudica. On arrival he quickly assessed the situation and judged it a hopeless cause. With only cavalry and a small local garrison available and in the absence of defensive walls it would be impossible to hold the town against the huge numbers coming to confront him.

London was a cosmopolitan merchant city which had grown rapidly in an uncoordinated way. It was free from the strictures of Roman planning and was an untidy town with a hotchpotch of buildings. Some were grand, built for well-to-do merchants, but these were jammed side by side with wooden shacks and sheds that not only were used for storage but for living quarters as well. Warehouses had been thrown up all along the riverside where cargo ships from around the empire jostled for position. London was prosperous and busy with an estimated population of between twenty and twenty-five thousand.

However, in the eyes of Boudica, London was Rome's creation and part of the hated occupation. No matter where the Londoners came from, they were all collaborators and sympathisers, so deserving of divine justice. Just like in Colchester a sense of dread filled Londoners as rumours circulated of the imminent arrival of the barbaric hordes. London had no barriers or defensive walls to speak of and for most there was no easy way to escape. A few rich merchants and officials such as the Procurator Decianus Catus had managed to commandeer boats and make off to the continent but there simply weren't enough ships for all.

With barbarians everywhere around London the countryside was full of danger too. When Paulinus arrived, he found the city full of foreboding. This turned to joy as word spread of salvation but rapidly turned to despair when Paulinus announced he was immediately leaving, not only with his cavalry but taking the local garrison with him as well.

Military commanders throughout the ages have had to make tough decisions, especially when faced with overwhelming odds and when placed in what they believe are completely indefensible positions. The sacrifice of the few to save the many is often trumpeted in military terms. However, in this case, the many of London and St Albans were to be sacrificed to save the few of Paulinus's immediate command and more generally ensure the survival of the Roman occupation of Britain and the governor's reputation.

All the governor could offer the terrified Londoners was a place in his retreating column, and only if they were able to keep up with it as it marched away. The garrison soldiers were fit young men who could cover twenty or more miles a day on foot carrying a full pack. Keeping up that pace would be impossible for most civilians except for the very fittest. Stragglers who fell by the wayside would be left behind. The Londoners who remained in the city because of their state of health, age or sex were left to their fate. Boudica's masses surged into London on the heels of the departing Suetonius Paulinus. There followed an orgy of destruction and unspeakable cruelty. The Roman writers gave graphic accounts. Tacitus stated the Britons were not interested in the 'commerce' of war.

> *For it was not on making prisoners and selling them or on any of the barter of war, that the enemy was bent, but on slaughter, on the gibbet, the fire and the cross, like men soon about to pay the penalty, and meanwhile snatching at instant vengeance. The Annals Book XIV 33*

For Boudica killing and burning was the order of the day and the more imaginative ways of dealing out death, so much the better.

Yet, whilst Boudica had destroyed London and later exacted a similar fate on St Albans, the Governor had managed to escape to fight another day. Boudica, for all the tactical skill she had shown up to that point, would regret the delay caused by the frenzy of destruction. It could even be said that by taking time out to destroy London and later St Albans, Boudica had suffered a tactical defeat. The effort spent in killing and burning could have been better used in pursuing and hunting down Suetonius Paulinus whilst he was weak and within rebel sights.

Boudica had missed the opportunity to cut the head off the Roman serpent.

Boudica's Nemesis

The orgy of destruction may have been Boudica's undoing. At this point we do not know if Boudica was still possessed by personal bloodlust or if her army was simply out of control and intoxicated by their so far easy victories. Without doubt maintaining discipline in the rebel ranks, made up of different tribes which until recently had been more than happy to fight each other, was an almost impossible task.

The rebels had no central command structure. Tribal loyalties would usually be to their own house, noble leader or strongman. Going to war was also a family affair. The men took their wives, children and even their domestic animals. Unlike the Romans the rebels had had no formal training. Their weapons were an ill assorted collection of make do. The tribal nobles may have had armour, a shield, perhaps a fine sword, a horse and even a chariot. The 'simple' men would have taken what they could find around their homes; hunting spears, homemade daggers, clubs and perhaps bows and arrows. More importantly the rebels received no pay and were uprooted from their homes and sustained only by common hatred of the enemy. Whilst they were away their crops would have withered in the fields.

As Paulinus retreated from London, the number of fighters in the field still gave Boudica a huge advantage. Paulinus left with his calvary, the London garrison and an unknown number of refugees. His thinking was that if he could link with up with the legions coming from Wales he could muster some 12,000 fighters. However, Boudica's pursuing army was estimated to be at least ten times that number.

None of the chroniclers record where Paulinus went after he left London other than that Boudica followed him which eventually led to the site of the final battle. All the while Paulinus was reported as having a great concern over his food supplies. He needed to feed not only his soldiers but the increasing numbers of refugees that had joined the column. First and foremost though, he needed sufficient provisions to keep his men fighting fit for the coming showdown.

Although the Roman forces retreated as quickly as possible, they were no doubt slowed by refugees. Boudica had her difficulties too. In East-Anglia she probably had some spies who could report on the movement of the IX Legion from Lincoln towards Colchester. However, unlike the Romans, the rebels had no countrywide 'intelligence' network that could track Paulinus as his legions marched away. It is also doubtful if the British tribes knew much or any of the geography of England outside their own tribal area. Even the most educated would be hard pushed to draw a rough map of southern England showing the principal towns and rivers, especially with so much of the land covered in forest.

Nevertheless, it seems that Boudica did track the Romans, following them as they moved away from London. As an army decamps, even the small one led by Paulinus, they would leave clues as to their route. Despite the best efforts to clear up, scattered around any stopping places would be signs of making and breaking camp, cooking fire remains, abandoned defensive dugouts and an assortment of discarded litter.

Yet, it is possible it was the Governor's master plan all along to leave clues for his enemy to follow to draw them into a trap. In fact, Paulinus may have already had a place in mind that was being prepared as the final killing ground.

Boudica's army was sustained by enthusiasm and an overwhelming desire to make the final kill but little else. Elements within it competed to be first to head the final charge. As they tracked Paulinus they came across cooking fires where the ashes were still warm. The rebels became ever more excitable as they felt the climax was imminent. They would exact revenge on the hated Romans and scourge them from their land.

Tacitus didn't identify the location of the final battle. He simply described it *as a place picked by Suetonius where the land narrowed* or in geographical terms a defile. The author Lewis Spence created a rough sketch map of the battle field (see page 61). No measurements were given but the area suggested could accommodate up to 150,000 fighters from two opposing sides. The battlefield sloped gently downwards and narrowed to the defile. On either side of the 'fighting area' was thick forest, or perhaps 2000 years ago high stony outcrops cut through by a river on one side. The Romans lined up in a defensive formation at the top the slope at its widest point with their rear protected by a tree lined ridge. To engage the Romans, the Boudican army would need to access the battlefield through a relatively narrow pass. Tacitus' description of the location of the climactic battle is in accord with the Governor's reputation as a master strategist.

The Roman legionnaires were massed six deep. On each side of the ranks were auxiliaries and units of cavalry. The rebels on exiting the defile would see from the bottom of the slope a line of Romans soldiers standing at the top. From the rebels point of view the Roman figures must have looked quite puny. However, the ranks standing behind the front line were hidden from view.

It would have been wise for Boudica to have reconnoitred the location more thoroughly and send scouts around the site and infiltrate the Romans through the flanks or from behind. Instead, Boudica led. According to Cassius Dio, she rode up and down the lines of rebels in her chariot urging them in a long speech to do battle and onwards to final victory.

Have no fear whatever of the Romans; for they are superior to us neither in numbers nor in bravery. Indeed, we enjoy such a surplus of bravery, that we regard our tents as safer than their walls and our shields as affording greater protection than their whole suits of mail. As a consequence, we when victorious capture them, and when overpowered elude them; and if we ever choose to retreat anywhere, we conceal ourselves in swamps and mountains so inaccessible that we can be neither discovered or taken. Our opponents, however, can neither pursue anybody, by reason of their heavy armour, nor yet flee; and if they ever do slip away from us, they take refuge in certain appointed spots, where they shut themselves up as in a trap. But these are not the only respects in which they are vastly inferior to us: there is also the fact that they cannot bear up under hunger, thirst, cold, or heat, as we can. They require shade and covering, they require kneaded bread and wine and oil, and if any of these things fails them, they perish; for us, on the other hand, any grass or root serves as bread, the juice of any plant as oil, any water as wine, any tree as a house. Let us, therefore, go against them trusting boldly to good fortune. Let us show them that they are hares and foxes trying to rule over dogs and wolves." History of Ancient Rome Book LXII

The rebels were impatient. Discipline had all but broken down. There is little in the way of battle description. The military historian James Maurice Scott suggested the Romans somehow provoked the rebels into recklessly charging.

Once the first of the rebels headed up the slope there was no holding back. Boudica's army pressed forward in a mad headlong rush filling the area of the battlefield. Facing them were disciplined Roman warriors. Each legionnaire carried two spears, a light and a heavy one. Once the rebels were in range, the first spears were thrown. The front rank then stepped back and was replaced by the second rank who turn were replaced by the third, fourth and fifth ranks.

Charging uphill was exhausting. Very soon there were so many rebel dead piled up in front of the Roman lines that those following had to climb over heaps of bodies to get at their quarry. This in turn made the Roman targets easier. Even for the toughest rebels the sight of so much carnage on their own side must have been unnerving. The rebel charge faltered. The Romans soldiers raised their shields, drew their short swords and sallied forth before dividing themselves into a series of wedges*. Now an unstoppable force was unleashed that hacked its way down the slope splitting the enemy ranks as they thrust forward. This was the Roman military way and a supremely efficient killing machine.

Hemmed in, the surviving rebels had little room for manoeuvre and began to panic and run, but there was no escape. Boxed in by the cavalry on either side, the rebel centre was cut to pieces. At the bottom of the slope the rebel wagons had been drawn up in a line to offer a viewing platform. The families, the spectators, had hoped to witness a spectacular victory. Instead, the line of waggons became a barrier barring the rebel fighters' escape. The Roman war machine advanced steadily and butchering their way through the fighters before moving on to kill the traumatised spectators without mercy, women, children, and animals alike.

Dio Casius described the sack of London in gory detail. Tacitus estimated the death toll in London, St Albans, Colchester, and the rout of the IX legion, at as much as 70,000. This figure included Roman citizens, their allies and all those caught in the middle, like the civilians that today would be described as collateral damage.

Assuming the figures are anywhere near accurate they are truly staggering in relation to the size of the English population.

**An offensive military formation formed to punch through enemy lines.*

An equivalent number today would equate to a death toll of three and a half million. Up to this point no figures were given for Boudica's losses although her army probably suffered substantial casualties when ambushing the Roman IX Legions sent to relieve Colchester.

With the conclusion of the final battle Tacitus then added to the above number and wrote, 80,000 Britons fell against the loss of only 400 Romans. For the Romans victory was complete. For the Britons in a space of a few hours their army had been destroyed.

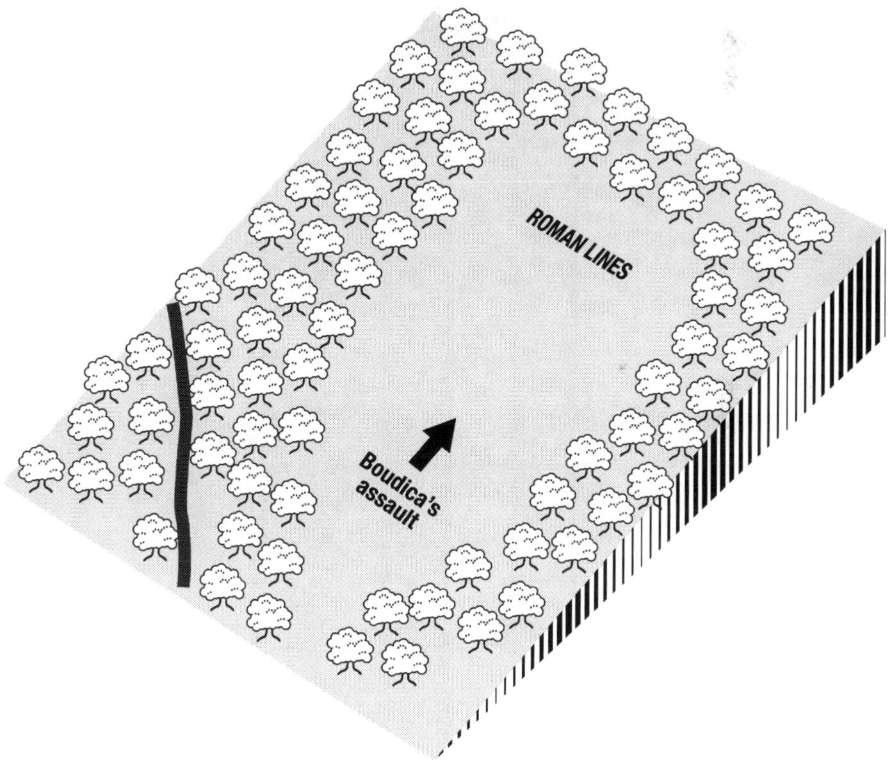

Scott's battlefield map. 2000 years ago the flanks may not have been trees but stony outcrops.

Thomas Thornycroft's Boadicea Group of Statuary
as it was known and erected in 1902 on the Embankment
opposite the Houses of Parliament

Johnathan Clarke's 1999 modern Boudica looking over Colchester North station
(see page 97)

The Final Battlefield?

Suetonius (the Roman Commander) chose a position approached by a narrow defile, closed in at the rear by a forest having first ascertained that there was not a soldier of the enemy except in his front, where an open plain extended without any danger from ambuscades. (Tacitus)

Unfortunately, the sparse description of the battlefield site above taken from the 1884 edition of *The Annals,* Book XIV (34) could theoretically apply to dozens of sites in the southern half of England.

On page 61 we showed an updated map of the battlefield taken from a sketch by James Maurice Scott. However, the local historian Margaret Hughes, in her 2020 book *Boudica at Mancetter,* has questioned the English translation of the above in respect of the word *defile* (a narrow pass). (Narrow) defile is an English translation of the Latin *artis facibus.* The root form of *facibus* is *faux* and mostly used in the form *fauces* which has several meanings in English such as gullet, neck, throat, or the palatine arches at the back of the mouth, the fauces. So whilst Scott's map is accurate in so far as the English translation is concerned if the Latin is further analysed there could be one or more defiles leading to the battle site.

Many theories as to the whereabouts of the battle site were put forward during the Victorian era when there was much renewed interest in Boadicea and great enthusiasm for archaeological digs. Yet, it must be added that many of the digs conducted did not have the best historical motives in mind but rather the enrichment of landowners who hoped to find valuable relics.

Speculation on the location of the site has ranged far and wide. Messing (near Tiptree) between Maldon and Colchester in Essex was suggested by the Rev. Henry Jenkins in his *Observations on the Site of Camulodunum* in 1842 for the *Journal Archaeologia*. In the 1890s Henry Furneaux, an Oxford Classical Scholar who specialised in studies of Tacitus, concurred. Messing translates to 'Mæcca's people' but an alternative is Maes(ing) a Saxon term meaning field of the battle plane. Messing is also close to the Rampart, a scheduled monument on Haynes Green Road in Layer Marney and the site of a former Roman encampment.

One of the Boudica's Obelisks in Upshire

Another Essex location suggested was Ambresbury Banks in Theydon Woods, Epping Forest. Ambresbury Banks are the site of a pre-Roman, Iron Age Hill Fort located at the highest point in the forest, 116m or 384ft above sea level. A little to the north and just west of Copped Hall two obelisks were erected in Upshire. These are said to commemorate the death of Boudica.

The first at Copped Hall Green is where, following the destruction of her army by Paulinus, Boudica escaped in her chariot and supposedly took poison. The second obelisk marks the spot where, allegedly, she died. Neither obelisk is marked in any way. It seems the obelisks were put up in the early 18th century under the direction of William Shenstone, the poet and landscape gardener, credited with influencing the layout and ornamentation of the nearby Warlies Park. It was only later during the Victorian era that the obelisks became associated with Boudica which in turn led to some maps being marked accordingly.

Kings Cross in north London was another site favoured by Victorian writers. The Romans had a large base in the vicinity of Barnsbury Square, Islington, just north of Kings Cross railway station. It was thought that if all the modern building could be stripped away the contours of the land could fit the battlefield description of Tacitus.

Other sites for this battle have ranged as far north-west as Chester and numerous places across the Midlands. However, there is a loose consensus amongst the more recent students of Boudica that by combining the writings of Tacitus with a detailed study of the military logistics for both sides, the site of the final encounter is somewhere on, or very close to, the current A5 (Watling Street) on its route between Towcester in Northamptonshire and Cannock in Staffordshire.

With the Roman Governor Paulinus retreating from London, constantly worrying about food supplies and burdened with refugees, it seems Chester would have been a destination too far. Also, the further north his relatively lightly armed group had moved the more the dangers of ambushes from angry Welsh rebels grew.

Kings Cross station in London

Kings Cross in London together with Messing and Epping in Essex can perhaps be discounted too. Both locations were considerably further for any Roman relief legions coming from North Wales to march. Furthermore, with Boudica's hordes massed in and around Epping Forest and north-east of London, for Paulinus there were dangers at every turn and much less time to plan a counter move.

As for Kings Cross, in the 2000 years since Boudica's revolt this area of London has seen centuries of construction and demolition in all shapes and sizes and the diversion of watercourses and extensive tunnelling for overground and underground railways. Of course, many items of archaeological interest including Roman artefacts have been discovered over the years but nothing to suggest it was the site of a major battle.

With regards to Messing in Essex, an archaeological evaluation on part of the Ramparts was conducted as recently as June 2018 by Dr Elliot Hicks, on behalf of the Colchester Archaeological Trust. Looking for Boudica was not part of the brief but the final report concluded that 'no archaeological remains were uncovered'. Again, at Ambresbury Banks in Epping Forest, several digs have been conducted but nothing to support a battle has been found.

This brings us back to the A5 (Watling Street). John Waite, writing in 2007 in his book *Boudica's Last Stand,* suggested the final battle was at High Cross (Veronis) which is now in Leicestershire. High Cross is at the junction of Watling Street, the A5, and the old Roman Fosse Way which runs south-west to Gloucester where the Roman II legion was based. Thus, High Cross would have been a good rendezvous point for the Roman forces evacuating from London, the reinforcements withdrawn from Wales and the II Legion summoned from Gloucester, which as we know failed to arrive. At or near High Cross detailed plans could be made by Paulinus with this combined force to take on Boudica's army, all the while assumed to be pursuing the retreating Roman London garrison heading north.

However, and more specifically, the nearby village of Mancetter, just over the border in North Warwickshire, is perhaps a more plausible spot for this final decisive encounter. Local researcher and historian Margaret Hughes, mentioned previously, has conducted in depth research and described the village's choice as a coming together of *the Latin, the Land, and the Logistics.*

The name Mancetter is descended from what the Romans called *Manduessededum* which has Celtic origins meaning horse chariot. The native horse chariots, one of the most iconic symbols of Boudica's Army were written about by Julius Caesar after his first forays into the British Isles. So, perhaps in Roman eyes the horse chariots symbolised the rebel cause and Boudica.

There was a Roman vexillation fort at Mancetter built by the Roman XIV (Gemina) legion about ten years before the Boudican revolt. The fort is now long gone and archaeological evidence suggests it is highly probable that it was dismantled by the Romans themselves before Boudica's revolt. Nevertheless the ridge on which it was built is described as a superb defensive position. The site is now partly occupied by Mancetter Church.

For the actual battlefield location itself, Graham Webster in his 1978 book *Boudica* suggested Mancetter and writes of 'a steep escarpment of several hundred feet above the River Anker caused by a fault line composed of quartzite, a rock which resists weathering'. Building on this Margaret Hughes has also advocated Mancetter. In the 2000 years since the revolt the landscape archaeology could have changed to become what it is today. With the help of LIDAR (Light Detection and Ranging) aerial mapping and an in depth study of the Latin text, Hughes suggests Mancetter could well match the all too brief description supplied by Tacitus at the beginning of this chapter, and more so if there was more than one defile. However, archaeological finds around the site are inconclusive. A Roman javelin head was uncovered but this could be dated from any time during the near 400 years of occupation. Additionally, a couple of pieces of horse's harness have been unearthed that resemble similar finds in Norfolk (Iceni territory). Yet finding simple harnesses do not indicate a battle took place. Watling Street was no doubt busy with civilian traders travelling from the south to the north on the newly constructed Roman road.

Another aspect to consider is that if a battlefield site based on the sketch by John Maurice Scott is anywhere near correct, Paulinus would be taking an enormous gamble in bottling up all his available soldiers in a location that if the battle went wrong there would be no escape.

For all the possible final battle sites considered, inclusion is simply based on supposition, built on supposition. In the nearly 2000 years that have elapsed since Boudica's revolt human activity has brought many changes to the landscape leaving evidence of past events yet to be discovered or simply buried forever.

Nevertheless, as part of their *Short Guide to Roman Mancetter* the Parish Council, in conjunction with Atherstone Civic Society, hopes to put up information boards for short walks, one of which will outline Mancetter's claim to being the site of Boudica's last battle.

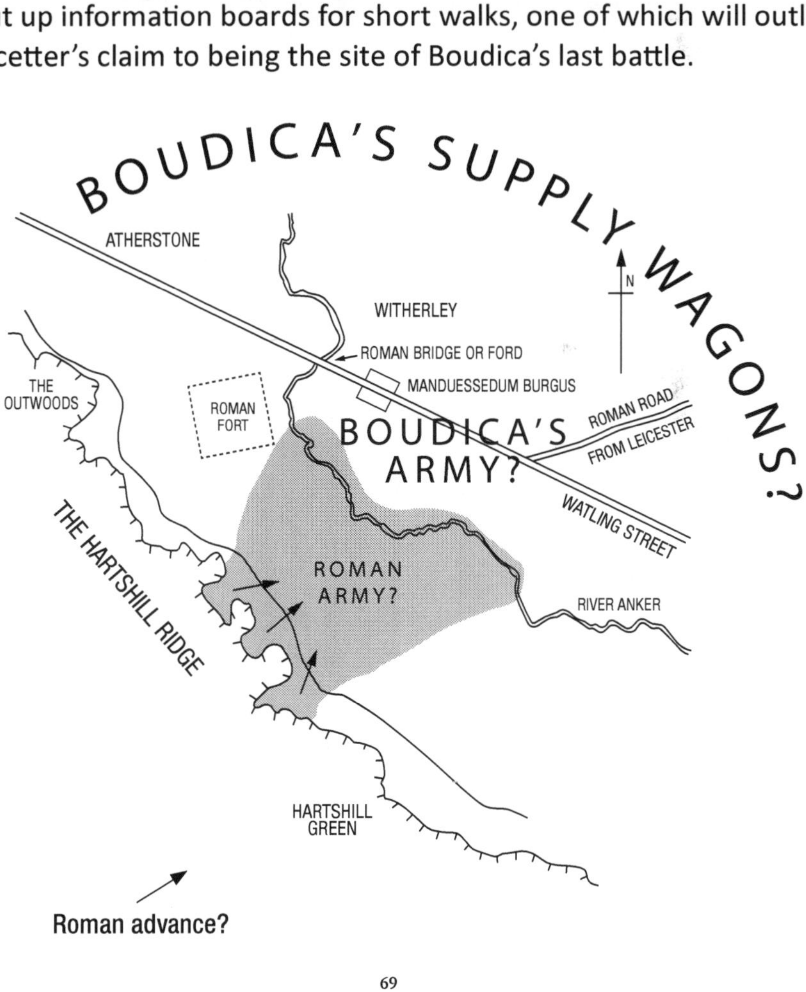

Aftermath

The revolt, the final battle and its aftermath, assuming the numbers were correct, saw the greatest ever slaughter the British Isles have ever known. The final battle itself, according to Tacitus, resulted in 80,000 British and 400 Roman dead. However, more was to follow.

Although Suetonius Paulinus had vanquished Boudica, he must have been outraged that the revolt had taken place under his watch. After all he had conquered Wales only to see his victory undone. Furthermore, in his view his opponent had not been an experienced general but just a minor tribal leader, in fact a nobody who also happened to be a woman. He was also angry that Boudica seemed to have escaped. She hadn't been killed on the battlefield or captured; thus, he was denied the pleasure of sending her in chains to Rome and parading his captive before the cheering Roman crowds.

With the Boudican army crushed and to satisfy his craving for vengeance Paulinus embarked on a genocidal mission to eliminate not only the tribes who supported the revolt but also those who had not actively sided with the Romans. The policy was vindictive and cruel in the extreme. The Trinovantes and the Iceni were especially singled out for punishment. The Trinovantes were the most exposed. They lived around Colchester, Chelmsford and London and were ruthlessly hunted down. In Roman eyes they were vermin.

With the onset of winter, the Roman legionnaires, who usually passed their time in comfortable winter quarters outside of the campaigning season, were ordered to pursue the scattered rebels into East-Anglia. The Iceni were harder to find. They had no large centres of population and lived in scattered communities in the marshes and fenlands. Iceni homes and farms that were found were put to the torch along with any food stores. Livestock was slaughtered or confiscated. It was the ultimate in scorched earth.

Despite the cold and rain, the Romans had plenty of incentive to seek out their quarry.

Those hunted could well have been responsible for outrages and the skewering of women on stakes during the rebels' attack on London. The hunters may have personally witnessed the aftermath of the atrocities committed or at least heard graphic accounts of the barbarism from their comrades. The harsh repression continued without let up for at least 18 months and the British Isles descended into chaos.

The disappearance of former Procurator Decianus Catus added to the confusion. He had taken with him his confidants and destroyed or lost most of the records. Sometime during AD61 a new Procurator was sent for from Rome, Julius Alpinus Classicianus. Classicianus was a Roman citizen but not from Rome. He came from Trier in present day Germany. Unlike his predecessor he was a man of integrity and of great moral courage. Classicianus was faced with the daunting task of rebuilding the civil administration. All the while the Governor's harsh repression continued which led to widespread famine.

The new Procurator was increasingly uneasy with Paulinus's continuing appetite for repression. Revenge and dented pride was one thing, perhaps to be commended, but continual destruction was no longer serving Roman interests. The British Isles were becoming a severe drain, not only on the local exchequer but that of Rome too. Afterall, Roman provinces were supposed to at least pay their way and even better return a profit.

The British Isles were potentially rich. Before the revolt Britain had productive agriculture, it exported corn, hides, dogs, horses and shellfish. There was great potential to exploit the mineral resources but to achieve this peace and stability were needed. Classicianus argued that starved, bankrupt or dead Britons had no economic value. Yet the Governor would not listen. As far as he was concerned there were still gangs of rebels on the loose and they must be eliminated.

Unable to persuade the Governor to change course, the Procurator wrote to Emperor Nero outlining his concerns in detail.

Nero was sympathetic but felt it unwise to recall a heroic military man as it would have caused outrage in Rome.

As a compromise, a Commission of Enquiry was set up led by a former slave called Polyclitus. Polyclitus travelled to the British Isles with a huge retinue of clerical and household staff. On arrival he began an extensive tour of inspection. In the report he sent to Rome he recommended that the war of attrition be ended and changed to one of construction and reconciliation.

Again, Governor Paulinus still refused to budge from what he saw as his divine mission of retribution. In the late summer of AD63 Nero found an excuse to recall Paulinus, following the mysterious loss of several ships and their crews in English waters during what may be guessed as being a botched raid on the Iceni. Without any fuss Paulinus returned to Rome neither in triumph nor disgrace.

By late AD63 the three principal actors in the revolt were gone. Boudica and her daughters were last seen galloping in their chariot, rousing the spirits of the rebels just before the final battle. Boudica is thought to have escaped to the Iceni homeland in East Anglia where she either died by taking poison or from hunger and disease. Procurator Catus fled to France and was never heard of again and Suetonius Paulinus had quietly returned Rome.

The revolt had cost upwards of 200,000 lives, combatants and civilians, through a combination of military action, revenge killing on both sides or famine caused by the repressive measures. These are truly horrific numbers considering the total population of Roman ruled Britannia was estimated as between half a million and a million.

After Paulinus departed, Rome took care in appointing the next Governor, Petronius Tupilianus. For the Empire it was economically vital to settle the disorder and end the killing. With Rome's new man in place, it is remarkable how quickly the province settled down. The remnants of the Iceni came out of hiding and began to rebuild their farms and sow their crops. *Pax Romana* was born again.

Petronius Tupilianus stayed in post for three years. The next Governor appointed, Trebillus Maximus, was a man without military experience.

For a short while the Roman Province of Britain enjoyed an unprecedented period of peace and the foundations of prosperity were laid. Much of the credit for the peace and reconstruction must be attributed to Procurator Classicianus. He inherited Catus's corrupt regime and set about building a new civil service of the highest standard of probity and justice. Little is known about Classicianus himself. He remained in office until AD65 and part of his tombstone, recovered in London, is on view in the British Museum.

So that's the substance of the story as far we know it but there are many unanswered questions which we can try and unravel in the following chapters.

Did Boudica's revolt achieve anything?

This is the perhaps the most important question. Did the revolt of Boudica's succeed in getting the Romans to leave? The insurrection lasted less than two years in one part of one Roman province during the nearly 1000 years of Empire. At its peak the Empire, (whose area was approximately half that of the USA) stretched 2,600 miles from the coast of Wales in the west to the Caspian Sea in Central Asia. The empire's northern frontier ran through Germany and Austria and onto the Black Sea, and then extended south to include the whole of the Mediterranean coastline.

The answer to the question, - *Did the revolt of Boudica's succeed in getting the Romans to leave?* must be a resounding no, since following the revolt the Romans remained in Britain for at least another 350 years. This may not be a long time in the development of a nation but it is still a significant amount of time. At the time of publication of this book if we go back 350 years, Charles II was King, Oliver Cromwell was not long dead, London had just endured plague and fire and Samuel Pepys was writing his diary. The nation was at war on and off with the Dutch over the spice trade. During one foray a Dutch fleet brazenly blocked the River Thames as far as Tilbury and then sailed down the River Medway and destroyed much of the English Fleet in Chatham. In East Anglia the Witch finder General, Matthew Hopkins, was at large seeking to send old ladies to the gallows and Isaac Newton was trying to work out gravity.

For nearly 400 years the Roman presence had a profound effect on Britain's development. Then it all came to an end with internal problems in Rome and the collapse of the Empire. All the garrisons were withdrawn from Britain to deal with problems closer to home. There was no insurrection in the British Isles to drive the Romans out or even to hasten their retreat.

Another question is, did Boudica's actions improve the lot of the English population? The answer too must be a no, especially in the short term. The death toll during the fighting was catastrophic and the revolt's aftermath saw Roman retribution, destruction and resultant famine on an unprecedented scale. In the longer term living conditions for the British did get better but only after the Romans realised that continual repression was not in their interests.

Gradually, as in other parts of the Roman Empire, the tribes in Britannia began to assimilate and Romanise themselves and take advantage of being part of the Empire. Again, we need to remind ourselves that before the Romans set foot in the British Isles the population was made up of an assortment of warring tribes who considered randomly attacking each other as the normal state of affairs.

Whilst there is no question that Boudica was severely and understandably provoked by the gangs of thugs from Colchester working for Procurator Catus, the revolt was nevertheless a retrogressive factor in that it slowed down the coming of what we might call civilisation to the British Isles.

In the British Isles today there are many reminders of the Roman presence. Roman walls and part buildings still stand. Decorative mosaics are still being discovered. Roman ornaments, pottery and statues unearthed to date have been restored as much as possible and such discoveries have been given pride of place in museums.

In contrast, Boudica and the Iceni have left little legacy. There are a few coins and some harnesses dating from the pre-roman era. Iceni chariots have been reconstructed. Some coins can be seen in the Norwich Castle museum. Yet, none of these coins can be connected to Queen Boudica. Sadly, the only other legacy that remains is layers of ash found below the three towns ransacked and burnt.

Despite this, over the centuries Boudica remains an excellent source for writers of fiction, speculation, and a subject for further historical investigation.

Following the revolt, Colchester, London, and St Albans were surrounded by defensive walls. Later Colchester was replaced by London as the provincial capital.

How do we know what we know?
The Enigma of the Writers

Before looking at the numerous puzzles at every stage of the Boudican revolt it would be useful to look at the original sources. This is a challenge. It is worth repeating that our knowledge of Queen Boudica's revolt is based on second hand accounts written many years after the event. There are two primary sources of 'the facts' both written by Romans or those in the employ of Romans, that is to say, all written by the winning side.

There are no contemporary English/British accounts of the revolt. It should also be born in mind that these primary sources were written respectively in Latin or Greek. The first is by the Roman historian Publius (or Gaius) Tacitus.

The second source published nearly 150 years later was by the Greek Roman historian, Lucious Dio Cassius, and written in Greek. Over the centuries their originals have been rewritten then retranslated and reinterpreted several times. The works have been regularly copied, perhaps inaccurately and with large parts missing.

During the infighting and power struggles of the Romans in the latter days of the Empire, plus the sacking of Rome by the Visigoths in AD410, much of classical Roman literature and histories were destroyed or simply disappeared.

Perhaps even stranger is that once the Roman Empire collapsed or ceased to exist the surviving manuscripts from Roman authors such as Tacitus lay undisturbed in store for hundreds of years before any great interest was taken in them.

Cornelius Tacitus (56AD to 117AD) is credited with writing amongst other works, *Agricola, Germania, the Histories* and *the Annals,* of which only half of the 30 volumes survived. Of the original handwriting of Tacitus or that of scribes in his employ, nothing remains intact, only fragments. What remains is contained on just two manuscripts created at least 800 years later. The first six books of the *Annals* were uncovered in a single manuscript written by unnamed monastic chroniclers in Germany in the Benedictine Abbey of Fulda before being transferred to the monastery of Corvey, in Saxony. This manuscript is now in Florence at the Laurentian Library or Bibliotheca Medicea Laurenziana. Another manuscript also now in Florence, part *Annals* and part *Histories,* was written or copied at Monte Cassino, again by unnamed chroniclers.

Dio Cassius, (155AD to 235AD) was born in what is now modern day Turkey. He moved to Rome in his late 20s. During his career as a Roman politician and administrator, he created some eighty volumes of history on ancient Rome covering roughly 1000 years from the 8th century BC until the 3rd century AD. Only about half of the books survive although there are fragments of others.

Currently the remaining manuscripts are shared between Italy and France. Dio Cassius's interpretation of the Boudican revolt rests in the Vatican Library in Rome but only a fraction of his works are contained there.

The early 1500s saw a huge surge of interest in the manuscripts of Tacitus which attracted the attention of the finest scholars of the time. On at least one occasion the 'Corvey' manuscript was stolen and then ransomed before coming into the possession of Pope Leo X. Even in the 20th century, during World War II, Adolf Hitler authorised commandos to seek out the manuscripts in Italy and bring them back to Germany.

The manuscripts were highly prized and the eminent classical scholar Doctor Clarence W. Mendell, of Yale, noted that since 1775 at least six attempts to discredit the works had been made describing them as forgeries or fiction. The French historian and philosopher Voltaire was the first to allege this and later Napoleon Bonaparte backed him, but overall, none of the arguments of forgery found acceptance among most scholars.

The golden age of Tacitean studies began with the posthumous publication, in 1515, of the works of Philippus Beroaldus, a professor at the University of Bologna. Thereafter for almost another 100 years many other scholars researched Tacitus and added their conclusions as to the meaning of his works, often disagreeing with each other on the finer meanings and nuances. Another surge of interest came in the Victorian and Edwardian era as British classical authors added to the interpretations of Tacitus.

Tacitus wrote in a very matter of fact way. However, Dio Cassius has been accused by successive scholars of gross exaggeration and creating speeches for the leading figures of the revolt to suit his narrative.

It must also be emphasised that Roman historians had to be very careful when recording events. If their version conflicted with the official views of the Emperor and his closest supporters, the consequences could be serious. Possibly at great risk, Tacitus documented the injustices suffered by the Iceni and Boudica at the hands of the Romans in some detail. However, both authors balanced their reports with graphic accounts of atrocities committed by Boudica's forces when they sacked Colchester and London.

Both writers produced a huge volume of work on the history of the Roman Empire and it is fair to say that their coverage of the revolt of Boudica was just a tiny part.

Unearthing the Evidence

To a certain extent the only real evidence that something cataclysmic took place 2000 years ago is from having dug down to find what is known as 'Boudica's or Boadicea's Destruction Horizon'. Digs have concluded that Colchester, London and St Albans were destroyed and burned to the ground. Excavations in all three locations have revealed thick layers of red soot, as well as artefacts showing evidence of severe scorching.

For a time a glass panel in the cellar of the George Hotel in Colchester's High Street was accessible to the public. It offered a chance to view this distinctive burnt red clay. However, this view is no longer available. Colchester Castle museum has an online collection dedicated to 'Boudica's Destruction of Colchester', which includes a section of a disfigured Roman stud-and-wattle wall from Lion Walk.

Found in the River Alde

In 1907, a life sized head of a bronze statue was fished out of the River Alde at Rendham, near Saxmundham in Suffolk (on the border of former Iceni territory). It was an archaeological find of great significance and was seized on by students of Boudica. Speculation was that it was the head of one of either of the Roman emperors Claudius or Nero and it was claimed that it had been torn down in Colchester by Boudica's victorious forces and then taken north to where it was vandalised and then ignominiously dumped.

The 'head' is now in the British Museum. Detailed analysis at the museum has found no evidence that the head was even linked with Colchester, let alone taken in triumph by Boudica's forces, or exactly whose head it is.

Finding the bodies

Apart from its location there is another major 'unknown' about the final battle. To date, no mass graves containing the remains of tens of thousands of bodies and their weapons, that might confirm its location, have been unearthed. Of course, over the course of two millennia it is possible all evidence of such a large battle, with a death toll numbering 80,000, may have disappeared. Yet this seems unlikely. Many remains such as skeletons from the Roman era (or before) have been unearthed during archaeological digs. It also seems implausible that with such a large death toll in a small area this gruesome event would be erased totally from the collective human psyche and not passed into local (English) folklore.

Cremation was a possibility. However, osteologists from the Museum of London Archaeology (MOLA) point out that cremating the numbers allegedly slain would be an undertaking of epic proportions. Enormous amounts of dry timber would be needed and elaborate pyres built on which to place bodies allowing for sufficient oxygen to flow for combustion. Even if this was done, after several hours and with constant feeding of the flames with additional fuel, skeletonised bodies would remain. Mass burial, another option, is also a major undertaking. This would require hundreds of slaves working under Roman supervision to dig the graves and bury the bodies.

It also seems doubtful that after his victory the Roman commander Suetonius Paulinus, still fearful of ambush from scattered rebels, would want his men to stay on the battlefield and oversee such a huge burial operation. Even if the Romans had managed to complete a mass burial of Boudica's defeated army, for the bones to remain undiscovered the depth of the graves would have to have been enormous.

Decomposition is influenced by a number of taphonomic factors that can speed up or slow down the decomposition process. Decomposition would be dependent on multiple variables including the acidity of the soil, bacteria within it, local temperature, humidity and insect and scavenger activity. Local fungi and vegetation would need to be assessed as would drainage and soil erosion. Another factor affecting decomposition is how densely packed the bodies were in the grave.

Of course, the dead could have been left where they lay to be scavenged away through the ages but then again such a brutal happening would be remembered and passed down through the generations. Also, to clear the battlefield the Romans would have needed to collect up every single discarded weapon, yet another major undertaking.

Historically, after battles the collection of the remains of bodies for burial or cremation would be undertaken by relatives or friends of the deceased. The bodies would be buried individually or returned to their place of origin. Accordingly, the battlefield location would be seared into the memory for successive generations. Yet with the writer Tacitus describing a complete annihilation of not only Boudica's fighters but all those watching too, returning the dead to their homeland would have been out of the question.

Were Colchester, St Albans and London completely destroyed during the uprising?

Research undertaken by MOLA between 2010 and 2013 may cast doubt on the severity of the destruction wreaked by Boudica on St Albans (Verulamium) and London (Londinium). Excavations in a dig in waterlogged ground beside the Walbrook River, the site of Bloomberg's European headquarters in the City of London, found the remains of hundreds of Roman waxed writing tablets of which approximately a quarter were readable.

The tablets provide a rare insight into how the city recovered after its destruction. At least one of the tablets could be historically significant in the context of the rebellion. Careful research has revealed them to be mostly legal and commercial documents related to people working in Roman London. Although very little is known about how soon London returned to normal, one of the tablets could be historically important.

It was a contract from 21st October AD62, only a year or two after the uprising, and it confirmed the order of *'20 loads of provisions' from St Albans to London.* This would indicate both cities were operating commercially to some extent shortly after the uprising, despite the ongoing campaign of Governor Paulinus to punish the indigenous population.

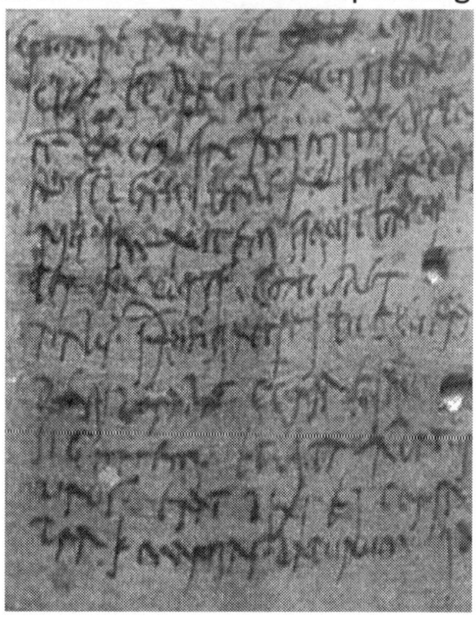

There are sadly no such indicators as to post rebellion trade in Colchester and no records of rebuilding the city. Also the vendetta of Paulinus against the rebels, firmly focussed on East Anglia, would presumably have discouraged trade.

Boudica's Assault on London

Although Boudica's attacks on Colchester and London are well documented in gory detail by the Roman writers, much detail is missing. There are no records of how and when her army travelled from Colchester to London. Unlike the Vikings who came 800 years later, Boudica's army, made up initially of the Iceni and Trinovantes peoples, had no ships. Dio Cassius wrote that her army initially numbered 100,000 and doubled in size by the time it reached London.

Without ships the best supposition is that the Boudican army travelled overland from Colchester, following the Roman or Great Road, roughly the route of today's A12. There were no other roads to speak of. Essex at that time was mostly forested. It is impossible to say just how good the Roman Road was between London and Colchester. The Romans had only been in England in force for 17 years and despite all the legendary Roman efficiency and mastery of construction it is difficult to believe a fully functioning road infrastructure was in place by AD60/61.

Today, for most of us travelling east or west across Essex, rivers such as the Blackwater, Chelmer and Wid are barely noticeable except for the odd sign on a bridge. These watercourses are regularly monitored for risk and embanked as needed but even in the 21st century during times of excessive rainfall overflows from the rivers can still cause severe flooding. However, for Boudica, every single river and stream, and there were many, would have presented a major obstacle and a huge logistical challenge for her army to cross. The map that follows shows the rivers of Essex and the Great Road running south west from Colchester. The rebels would have had to cross at least five rivers before even getting to the outer London area.

Once the Boudican army entered the London area, the difficulties would have multiplied. Like much of the rest of Essex, Havering and Redbridge were forested. Apart from the Great Road to Colchester just a few tracks wound their way through the trees. There were two more relatively small rivers to be contended with, the Ingrebourne and the Rom/Beam. The areas in the south of Dagenham, Barking and Newham (that later became known as the levels) were mosquito infested marsh, subject to regular flooding, and consequently would have been impossible for a large army to cross quickly. Closer to the city the Rivers Roding and Lea would have been major obstacles, not only for people but also for fighting chariots, baggage wagons and pack animals. These rivers were not the tightly embanked waterways of today. There were no bridges. The first recorded bridge at Bow over the River Lea was built in about AD1100, one thousand years after Boudica's uprising.

The rivers Roding and Lea grew and shrank over wide flood plains with the tides and seasons. There were extensive marshes either side of the watercourses covering much of present day Stratford, Leyton and Barking and all the way down to the north bank of the River Thames. Also, in AD 60/61 there were no known flood defences for the River Thames thus huge swathes of land north of the river were prone to flooding.

Even today, despite vastly improved and coordinated flood prevention measures all along the Thames and the building of barriers, the risk of flooding is always present. Just to emphasise the size of the Rivers Roding and Lea in times past, 800 years after Boudica the Vikings sailed fleets of ships up both rivers to strike inland and as recently as the late 18th century the River Roding at Barking was home to the largest fishing fleet in the British Isles.

In examining the attack on London, it is assumed Boudica's assault took place in the spring or the summer, the so called fighting season. Yet this is just supposition. The Roman writers leave no clue as to the timing of the London assault or to the route taken from Colchester to London and it is not known in what condition or how wide the Roman (or Great Road) was.

This then poses another question. How long would it take for an army of one to two hundred thousand, mainly on foot, to march to London? *See maps overleaf*

Did Boudica travel to London by this route?

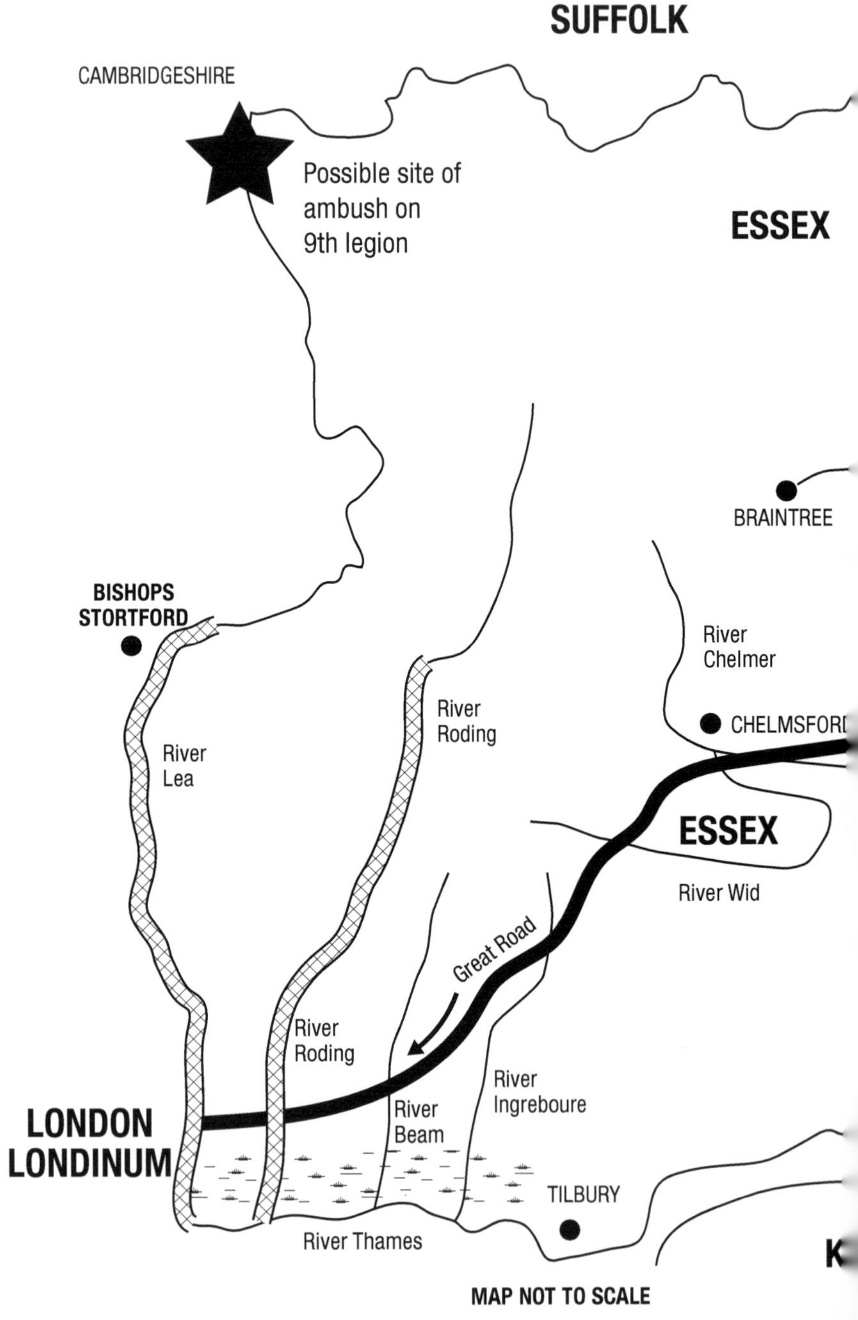

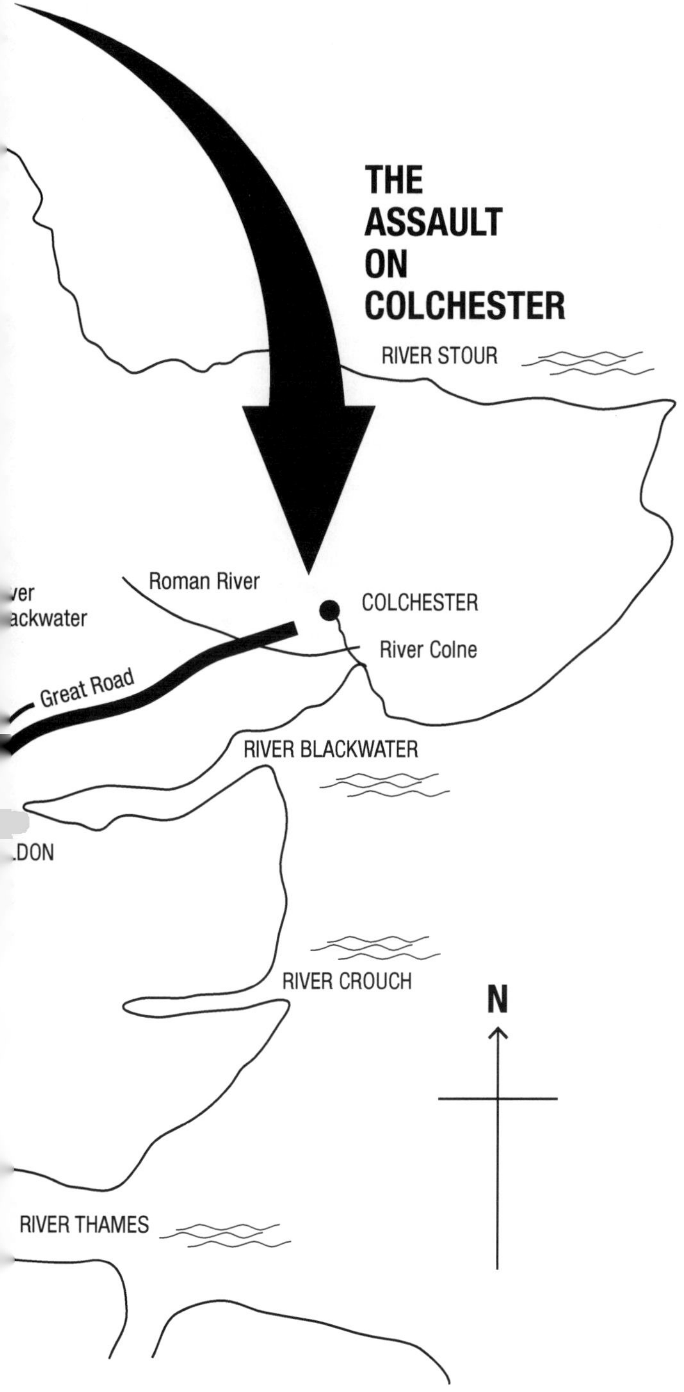
THE ASSAULT ON COLCHESTER
RIVER STOUR
Roman River
COLCHESTER
River Colne
Great Road
RIVER BLACKWATER
RIVER CROUCH
N
RIVER THAMES

An Alternative Route via Stane Street?

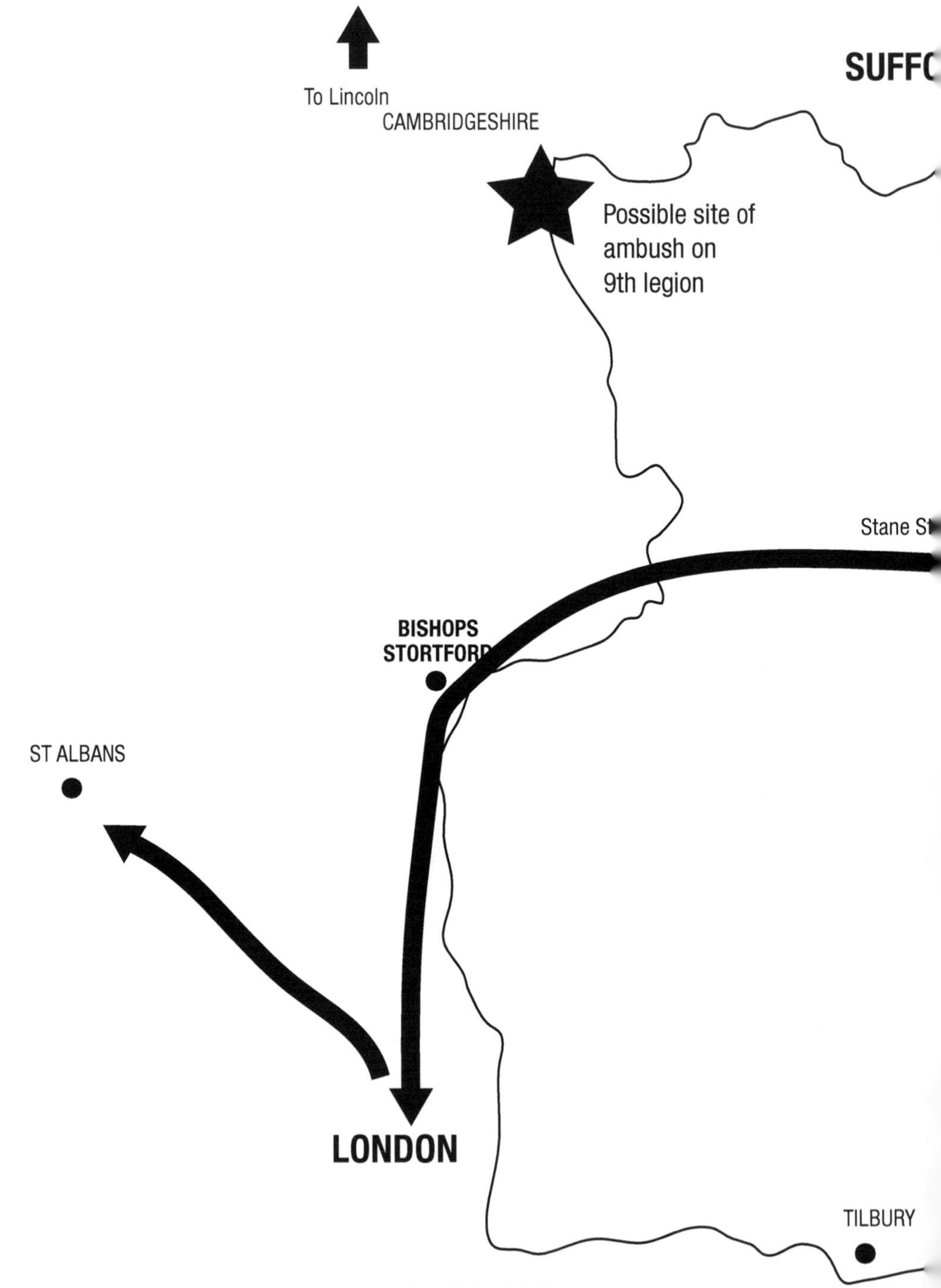

MAP NOT TO SCALE

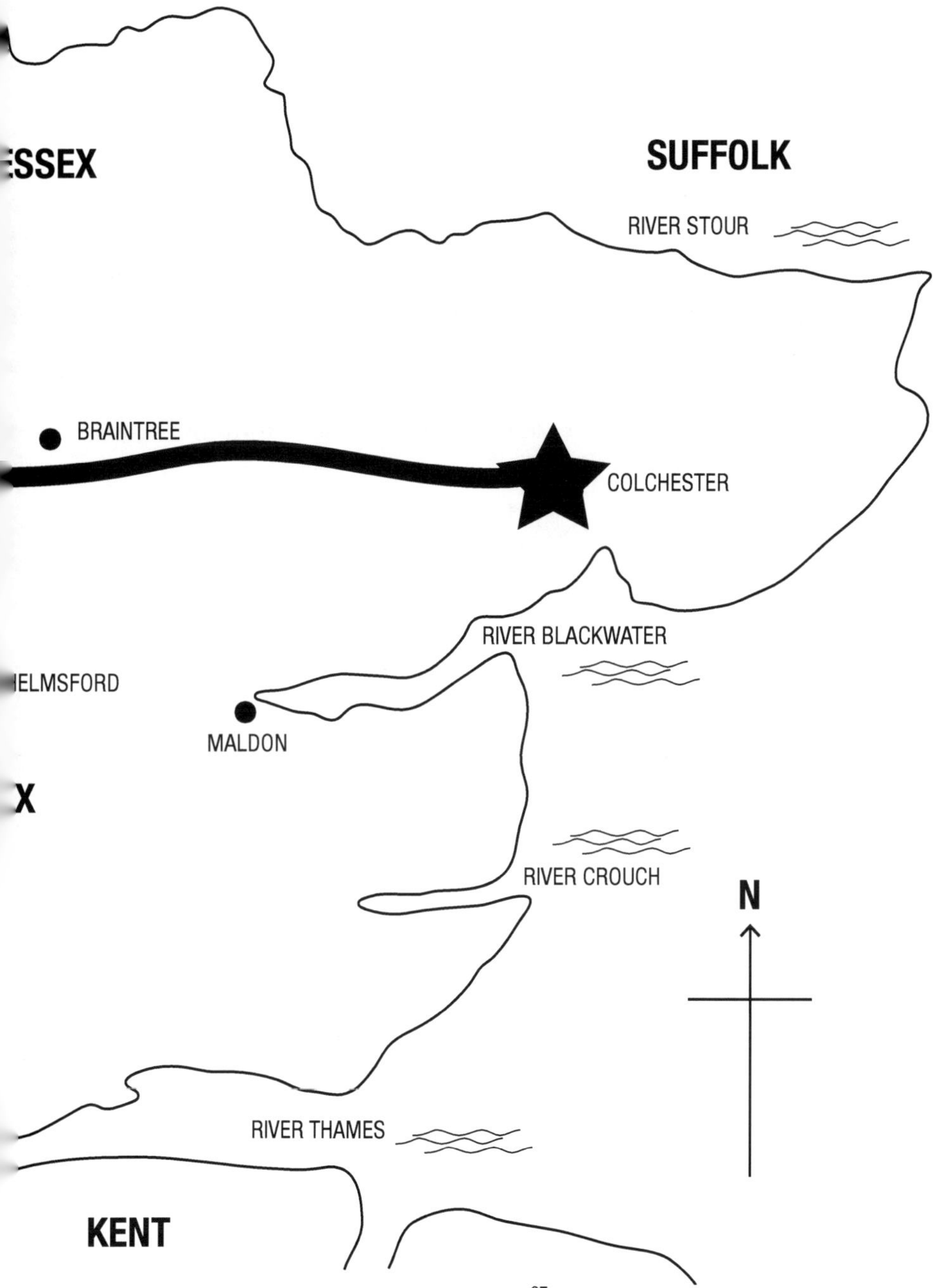

ESSEX
SUFFOLK
RIVER STOUR
BRAINTREE
COLCHESTER
RIVER BLACKWATER
ELMSFORD
MALDON
X
RIVER CROUCH
N
RIVER THAMES
KENT

Continued from page 83

Logically, the Governor's frantic gallop to London and subsequent withdrawal of the local garrison would imply that Paulinus was already aware of Boudica's decision to attack London immediately following the destruction of Colchester and the IX legion.

However, on Boudica's part there could have been little advance planning for this overland journey of about 60 miles. To the reader the distance may not seem a long way today. As mentioned, the route from Colchester to London was but a single road weaving its way through forest. The rivers would have slowed progress further so it is conceivable that the vanguard of Boudica's army could have arrived close to London whilst the rear guard was still departing from Colchester. Alternatively, if the rebels had delayed their march on London the Romans would have had time to organise the city's defences.

Whatever the case, military commanders since time immemorial have said that armies march on their stomachs, so how did Boudica gather all the food and supplies required for such vast numbers in such a short space of time and transport it? War chariots seem hardly suitable vehicles to be used as baggage wagons.

As for Boudica's direction of travel to London there is another possibility, see pages 86/87. After defeating the IX Legion en-route from Lincoln, possibly somewhere near Cambridge, Boudica's army could have assaulted London from the north, first by travelling west along what was known as Stane Street via Braintree, (roughly the route of the A120) before striking south. What also confuses matters further is that it is not known whether all of Boudica's available forces ambushed the IX legion or just some of them.

The route via Stane Street is also a much longer route and if this was the chosen line of attack, striking from the north, Boudica's forces could well have run into the Roman garrison withdrawing from London which surely would have been reported by the writer Tacitus.

Communications

Another aspect of Boudica's campaign and significant in all matters military is communications. For Boudica's assault on Colchester and London to have succeeded in the way the Roman writers described, good communications between the native tribes would have been essential along with a working chain of command.

There are no written records from the days of the Iceni or Trinovante so all communication would have been oral. We are left to wonder if the Iceni and Trinovantes spoke the same language or the same as the Catuvellauni who joined the fray later. Different tribes speaking different languages would seem to make military planning and arranging logistics on the scale required almost impossible. Of course it is possible that in the seventeen years of the Roman occupation some of the Iceni, the Trinovante and Catuvellauni could have learnt sufficient Latin to communicate with each other that way.

How many rebels were there?

Another puzzle is the size of the rebel army. Can the accounts by the Roman writers as to the numbers in Boudica's Army be given any credence? Rebel numbers are quoted as being between 100,000 and 230,000 and of 80,000 being killed during the final battle.

There are no reliable estimates for the size of the English population before 1801 when the first census was undertaken. This calculated the UK population in 1801 at just over nine million. Analysis of the Domesday Book (compiled around 1068) suggests a population of less than two million in England. As Boudica's revolt took place 1,000 years earlier it would not be unreasonable to believe the 'English' population would have been far smaller.

So, if the rebel numbers given by Dio Cassius are to be believed, it would seem virtually the whole population of England, men, women, and children would have been in Boudica's Army.

Yet, the rebel forces initially were drawn from East Anglia which even today is one of the least densely populated areas of England. With East Anglia being the home of the Iceni and Trinovante tribes, the Roman account of the numbers appear at best grossly exaggerated, or on the other hand completely implausible.

A question of numbers. Boudica heading her Army, but just how many were there?

Part II

Heritage, Legacy and Mythology

Despite the paucity of original detail about Boudica provided by the Roman writers, a simple internet search reveals nearly four million results. However, trawling through these is not particularly productive as any serious non-fiction examination of the results will lead back to the two original Roman sources.

The Boudica/ Boadicea images we are familiar with today were created at least 1700 years after the revolt. Of the numerous images available one of the earliest (see inside front cover) is called *Boadicea Haranguing the Britons.* It is an engraving by William Sharp based on a portrait by John Opie dated 1793.

Perhaps the most famous is the sculpture of Boadicea on her chariot with her daughters opposite the Houses of Parliament shown on page 62. The sculpture was created during the Victorian era. With British power, in the form of Empire, expanding rapidly throughout the world glorious icons were sought. The Victorians were masters at creating heritage often with scant relation to the facts. The statue of Boudica is no exception. The commission was awarded to Thomas Thornycroft. Thornycroft already had a record of creating fine works. Two of his sculptures are in the House of Lords. They are of Henry de Bohun and Roger le Bigod, two of the powerful Barons charged with enforcing the terms of the Magna Carta during the reign of King John.

The prime mover of awarding the commission was Prince Albert (the German husband) of Queen Victoria. Albert had been pleased with an equestrian statue of his wife made by Thornycroft. Again, to reiterate, this was now 1800 years after the revolt.

Thomas Thornycroft began work on the Boadicea statue. Prince Albert was reported as offering horses from the royal stables to use as models. Prince Albert though was not a well man and he died, possibly of typhoid, in 1861 at the age of 42. Queen Victoria went into prolonged mourning and royal interest the Boadicea sculpture waned. Thomas Thornycroft, the sculptor, then died in 1885 and the finished statue lay forgotten in storage.

Edward VII came to the throne in 1902 following the death of his mother Queen Victoria. Edward naturally wanted to mark his coronation with impressive monuments and had a desire, of course, to project British power during the golden days of Empire.

Thomas Thornycroft's son, who had been minding Boadicea's statue, arranged for it to be given a bronze coating. After several delays, following arguments as to where it should be located, the statue was handed over to the London County Council as a free gift by a 'small group of private citizens' headed by Mr William Bull the Member of Parliament for Hammersmith. *The Boadicea Group of Statuary,* as it was known in 1902, was then put up on Westminster Bridge opposite the Houses of Parliament where it remains today.

Perhaps the ultimate irony is that a statue, which celebrates - if that's the right word - a woman who burnt the city down and massacred all its inhabitants was put up opposite the Houses of Parliament, the heart of the British establishment.

Tacitus, the Roman author and source of much of the Boudican story was perhaps four or five years old when the revolt broke out. Some 40 years later his book *Agricola* was published, followed by another, the *Annals of Ancient Rome*. *Agricola* is a semi-biographical account of Julius Agricola, a Roman Officer who served under Governor Suetonius Paulinus throughout the revolt.

At least with Tacitus we can say he knew someone, Agricola, who was present when the revolt took place and may have seen action fighting Boudica. Agricola, some years later, became governor of Britain. Tacitus also married Agricola's daughter. Yet, extremely little is known of the writer's life or origin. He was born into a well to do family and received a good education which opened up the way for progression in Roman society. Tacitus served as a senator, later becoming a Consul in Rome and then moving on to the climax of his career as Governor of Western Anatolia (Turkey).

Cornelius Tacitus. The original source of much of the Boudica story. His statue is on the steps of the entrance to the Austrian parliament in Vienna.

Yet, there is no evidence that Tacitus ever visited Britain. His statue opposite is on the upper steps of the Austrian Parliament building in Vienna.

Back again to the Victorians. Queen Victoria came to the throne in June 1837 and six months later the cartoon below appeared in the *Tickler* magazine published by Sherwood, Neely and Jones. It shows Queen Victoria in the form of Boadicea on a chariot, leading in chains John Russell, the then Home Secretary, and Daniel O'Connell, described as the (Irish) liberator during the time of the so called tithe wars in Ireland.

Colchester Town Hall was opened a year after the death of Queen Victoria. Construction of the new building, designed by John Belcher, began in 1897 and was opened by the former Prime Minister, the Earl of Rosebery, in 1902. The town hall has a number of features referencing the rebellion which include a Boadicea stained glass panel in the Moot Hall (page 103). The panel is part of the Queen's window, made by the renowned London glass makers Clayton and Bell.

The window was presented, on behalf of the Ladies of Colchester, by Emily F. Sanders, the Mayoress and president of the committee. Inside the town hall council chamber is another window dedicated to the Roman Emperor Claudius, responsible for the AD43 invasion that subjugated Britannia to over 300 years of Roman rule. Another panel in the Moot Hall shows the rebel Caratacus.

On the exterior of the town hall one of the stone sculptures is of Boadicea, made by local stone maker L. J. Watts. (Front cover). Once again these are strange choices for the city fathers of Colchester to make. On one hand they commemorate the man responsible for the invasion and occupation of the country for 350 years, then on the other, the woman responsible for the town being burnt to the ground. Colchester Town Hall was completed in the same year as the Boadicea chariot statue was erected on the Thames embankment in London.

There are many other Roman statues around the country. Notably, Gaius Suetonius Paulinus, (Page 38) the Roman Governor and Commander who vanquished Boudica, can be seen on the terrace of the Roman Baths, in Bath.

The remains of the Roman Baths were only uncovered in 1878. They were subsequently explored by Major Charles Davis, the city surveyor architect. Just over 20 years later the baths, having been 'restored' as a visitor attraction, were officially opened to the public in 1897 by Prince George, the Duke of Cambridge. The statute of Gaius Suetonius Paulinus, sculpted by George Anderson Lawson, is one of nine on the upper terrace which include Julius Caesar, the governors Scapula and Agricola and Emperor Hadrian. The statues were carved in 1894.

Opposite Colchester's North Station, a modern sculpture of Boudica stands in the middle of a roundabout. It was jointly commissioned by a local supermarket and the City & Council Developments in 1999. This modern effigy was created out of aluminium armour by Johnathan Clarke (see page 63).

The sculpture is over five metres tall. Her outstretched shield and gravity-defying hair have been described as giving her an air of invincibility!

Celebrating Boudica continued well into the Edwardian era. Boadicea was adopted by the Suffragette movement. *The Bystander* magazine of April 1908 showed an image of the leading suffragette, Dame Christabel Pankhurst, by Richard George Mathews, where Pankhurst was described as *A Boadicea of Politics.*

Boudica was also adopted by the Suffragettes as one of their campaign symbols for women's suffrage. In 1908, a "Boadicea Banner" was carried in several marches of the National Union of Women's Suffrage Societies.

Another impressive sculpture of Buddug / Boadicea with her two daughters can be seen in Cardiff City Hall in Wales. This work again was created nearly 2000 years after the revolt. Work on the sculpture began in 1912. The sculptor chosen was James Havard Thomas. The finished marble figure, unlike that of Thomas Thornycroft's dashing work on the embankment in London, is a gentler work.

It depicts Boudica as a mother embracing her two daughters although the message is the same as Thornycroft's in that it is an appeal for Britons to avenge the wrongs done to her country and home. The Cardiff sculpture was financed privately and officially unveiled by the Secretary of State for War and soon to be Prime Minister David Lloyd George in October 1916.

Film and Television

In respect of film and television, and unlike the adventures of Robin Hood, the legendary English outlaw who stole from the rich and gave to the poor, this media has produced little on Boudica. This is possibly because there was no happy ending to the Boudica saga whichever way the story is spun.

Apart from several history themed television documentaries the only notable movie to have made it to the big screen is the 2003 film *Boudica* (or *Warrior Queen* in USA) featuring Alex Kingston.

After the film was completed Boudica's chariot was given to Colchester Castle Museum, although following a later museum renovation the film chariot was disposed of.

The scythes added to the wheels of the chariot as seen on Thomas Thornycroft's Statuary on the Embankment in London were all part of Victorian imaginative thinking rather than having a basis in fact.

Conclusion

It's fair to say that if hadn't been for two Roman authors, Tacitus and Dio Cassius, and a surge of interest some 1000 years later by medieval researchers based in what is now Italy, it is unlikely that in Britain today there would be any knowledge of Boudica or her rebellion. Even Cassius Dio ended his commentary on the revolt with the words, *So much for the affairs in Britain* (Book LXII 12.1), dismissing the uprising as almost a non-event in the Roman Empire's long history.

With many details missing from the two original sources; both written long after the event, it is even possible, no doubt much to the disappointment of many, that there was no such queen as Boudica and no such rebellion on the scale described.

We cannot know what the authors' motivations were in writing their histories. Who commissioned them? Were they required by the politics of the day to reinforce the power of the empire? Nevertheless, they are the only known near contemporary sources of the event.

The medieval researchers, no doubt much as later writers did, established tiny elements of 'fact' and made their suppositions according to the needs of the prevailing culture. Over the years, layer upon layer of suppositions have led to a whole range of possibilities to suit the prevailing needs of governments, particularly in the Victorian age, to reflect the power of Britain and its empire.

In the absence of any conclusive evidence such as the final battlefield site being discovered with evidence of the remains of 80,000 slain warriors or their weapons, or, even more unlikely, additional text emerging that can be authentically traced back two thousand years, the Boudica story is neatly summed up by John Waite's conclusion of his introduction in his book *Boudica's Last Stand;* 'Ultimately, whatever direction the researchers of the future take, the real treasure will lay with the first exciting discovery of solid irrefutable evidence which, if it is out there waiting to be found, eventually leads us to the truth. Wherever it may be.'

Thus Boudica, or Boadicea, as a queen, a mother and a warrior is likely to remain a historical mystery for the foreseeable future.

And The What If? Question

Boudica's revolt took place in AD60 or 61, we can't be sure which, but we know it was comprehensively defeated. Our *What If?* question is what would have been the outcome if the revolt took place eight or nine years later in AD 69 during the year of four emperors in Rome.

By AD68 Emperor Nero, who had overseen the defeat of Boudica, was universally despised. The senate declared him a public enemy. Nero fled Rome with a death sentence hanging over him and he committed suicide. This began an immense power-grab.

Nero was replaced by Servius Sulpicius Galba who had a reputation for greed and cruelty. Galba, once installed as Emperor, was faced with mutinies by the legions in Upper Germany. Galba was in poor health. He too soon became universally hated and in January of AD69 he was murdered by his guard. Galba was replaced as Emperor by Marcus Otho who was indignant that he had been passed over previously. Otho survived just three months. His attempt to quell the mutinies in Upper Germany, which were led by Aulus Vitellius, ended in failure. Like Nero, Otho committed suicide rather than continue to fight on.

In Cologne, in April of AD69, Vitellius was proclaimed the third Roman Emperor of that year. However, in July, Vitellius learned that the Eastern armies had proclaimed their commander, Titus Flavius Vespasianus, as emperor as well. Vitellius then sent his legions to do battle but they were decisively defeated. In the autumn Vespasian's troops entered Rome which resulted in widespread death and destruction in the city. According to Tacitus, Vitellius was dragged from his hiding place and killed by a mob who then threw the corpse into the River Tiber.

In December AD69 the Roman senate declared Vespasianus as Emperor. The year of the four emperors closed and the Vespasian dynasty began and lasted for 27 years.

So, what would have been the outcome if Boudica's rebellion had taken place in AD69 when Rome was in chaos, convulsed by infighting and even some of the legions in Britannia had been withdrawn to join the fray? ***What if?***

Who were the Druids?

As mentioned in the chapter, *The Roman Campaign in Wales,* beginning on page 43, the Druids were influential in stirring up resistance against Roman rule and occupation particularly in the west of England, the counties bordering Wales and of course Wales itself -but who were the Druids?

The origin of the word 'Druid'' is unclear but the most popular view is that it comes from 'doire', an Irish-Gaelic word for oak tree (often a symbol of knowledge), also meaning 'wisdom'. Druids were concerned with the natural world and its powers and considered trees especially sacred.

Druids were scattered across ancient Britain and France and reputed to be philosophers, teachers and judges. Supposedly the Druids collectively possessed a store of communal wisdom about the natural world and the ancient traditions of the peoples and acted as a conduit between human beings and the gods.

Almost everything known about the Druids is second-hand knowledge and texts that survive were written by non-druids. Much like the Boudican story, Romans have been the principal source. Julius Caesar was one of the foremost creators of druidic knowledge following his conquests in mainland Europe. Caesar was quoted as saying Druids preferred oral teaching to writing.

The Roman destruction of the Druid's sacred groves on Anglesey is highlighted by both authors Tacitus and Dio Cassius. Yet it is not clear what the groves were. The Welsh Ynys Mon, (Anglesey) translates as the land of the apples. Quite how far back Anglesey has been associated with apples is unclear. Some tree species on Anglesey are thought to date back over 1000 years, although this is still 1000 years after Boudica's time. However, whether apple trees were part of the Druid sacred groves is open to speculation. Other explanations of Druid sacred groves are that they were simply enclosed secret spaces where the Druids practiced their rituals.

Nevertheless, it seems fairly certain that Druids were revered and inspirational for early opposition to Roman rule in Britain, although there and then again what hold or influence the Druids had on Boudica is completely unknown.

An Arch Druid in his Judicial Habit

Over the years Druids are quoted in many exaggerated magical and mystical tales. It is virtually impossible to separate fact from fiction.

As a strange aside the former Prime Minister Winston Churchill was inducted into the Albion Lodge of the Ancient Order of Druids at Blenheim in August 1908.

The stained-glass window featuring Boadicea in Colchester Town Hall

About the Author

Andrew Summers was born within the sound of Bow Bells (on a quiet day) and after a spell in North Kent has lived in Hadleigh in Essex for the last 35 years and been married to Glenis for over 50 years. Andrew has bought books, sold books, printed books and now writes and publishes books too!

Andrew has edited *The Numbers Had to Tally,* a Second World War survival story and *Once Upon a Time in Southend (and District).* He has also penned *They Did Their Duty, Essex Farm,* a book which tells the story of Essex Farm in Belgium and its connections with the Essex Regiment.

Along with his colleague John Debenham, Andrew has co-authored several books in the Essex Hundred series such as *The Essex Hundred Histories, The Essex Hundred,* (The History of Essex in 100 poems), *Battlefield Essex* and *Magna Carta in Essex*.

Andrew is still busy writing and pandemics permitting tours the county giving talks on a variety of Essex topics.

A list of books available from Essex Hundred Publications at the time of *The Riddle of Boudica* going to press to can viewed from page 114 onwards.

Alternatively check out www.essex100.com

Places of Interest

British Museum
Great Russell Street,
London, WC1B 3DG
https://www.britishmuseum.org/

Colchester Castle Museum
Castle Park,
Colchester CO1 1TJ
https://colchester.cimuseums.org.uk/visit/colchester-castle/

In AD49, Colchester was the first place in Britannia to be given the status of a Roman Colonia. A Colonia was a planned settlement for retired veteran soldiers who became citizens of Rome upon discharge, with all the privileges that Roman citizenship afforded. Nearly 2000 years later In 2019 Colchester Borough Council put up new Welcome signs.

Colchester Town Hall
High Street, Colchester, CO1 1PJ
https://www.colchester.gov.uk/

Lunt Fort
Coventry Road, Baginton,
Warwickshire, CV8 3AJ
https://www.luntromanfort.org

Museum of London
150 London Wall, London
EC2Y 5HN
www.museumoflondon.org.uk

Norwich Castle Museum & Art Gallery
Castle Hill, Norwich, NR1 3JU
https://www.museums.norfolk.gov.uk/norwich-castle

Roman Baths
Abbey Church Yard,
Bath, BA1 1LZ
https://www.romanbaths.co.uk/

Roman Mancetter
& Boudica Heritage Centre
St Peters Church,
Mancetter Road, Mancetter,
Atherstone, CV9 1NH
https://www.romanmancetter.org.uk/

Verulamium Museum (St Albans)
St Michael's, St Albans, AL3 4SW
https://www.stalbansmuseums.org.uk/visit/verulamium-museum

Wall Roman Site
Watling St, Wall,
Lichfield, WS14 0AW
https://www.english-heritage.org.uk/visit/places/wall-roman-site/

Selected Bibliography

Addison, William, Sir, *Epping Forest, Figures in a Landscape*, Robert Hale, 1991

Aldhouse-Green, Miranda, *Bog Bodies Uncovered, Solving Europe's Ancient Mystery,* Thames & Hudson, 2015

Bahn, Paul, consultant editor, *Written in Bones,* Quantum, 2002

Bédoyère, Guy De La, *The Real Lives of Roman Britain,* Yale University Press, 2016

Piggott, Stuart, *The Druids,* Thames and Hudson, 1968

Davis, Hugh, *Roman Roads in Roman Britain*, Tempus Publishing, 2002

Cunliffe, *Barry, Druids a Short Introduction*, Oxford, 2010

Hingley, Richard & Unwin,Christina, *Boudicca, Iron Age Warrior Warrior,* Hambeldon & London, 2005

Hoy, Ken, *Getting to Know Epping Forest*, The Old Beerhouse, 2002

Hughes, Margaret, *Boudica at Mancetter: The Latin, The Land, The Logistics,* Atherstone Civic Society, 2020

Kemble, James, *Prehistorical & Roman Essex,* Tempus, 2001

Scott, J.M., *Boadicea, Queen of the Iceni who died in AD61 after leading her people against the Roman Invader.* Constable, London, 1969

Scullard, H.H., *Roman Britain, Outpost of the Empire.* Thames & Hudson, 1986

Spense, Lewis, *Boadicea, Warrior Queen of the Britons,* Robert Hale Ltd., 1937

Waite, John, *Boudica's Last Stand, Britain's Revolt Against Rome*, AD 60-61

Continued over

Classical Sources

Cassius, Dio, *Roman History*, Loeb Classical Library, Heinemann, 1913

Goodyear, F.R.D., *The Annals of Tacitus Vol 1 (Annals I. 1-54)* Cambridge University Press, 1972

Tacitus, *Agricola and Germania.* (translated by Harold Mattingly*),* Penguin, 1948

Tacitus, *The Dialogus of Publius Cornelius Tacitus* (translated by Sir William Peterson), William Hienemann, 1932

Tacitus, *The Histories*, Wellesley Kenneth, Rhiannon Ash, Penguin,1964

Tacitus, *The Annals of Imperial Rome,* Translated by Michael Grant, 1956, (reprinted 1996 with revisions), Penguin Books

Walker B., *The Annuals of Tacitus, A Study in the Writing of History,* Manchester University Press, 1952

Online

Colchester Castle Museum collection dedicated to 'Boudicca's Destruction of Colchester
https://colchester.cimuseums.org.uk/visit/colchester-castle

University of Warwick
https://warwick.ac.uk/fac/arts/classics/warwickclassicsnetwork/

Perseus Digital Library (USA)
http://www.perseus.tufts.edu/

The Gardens Trust
https://www.essexgardenstrust.org.uk/s/Warlies.pdf

Index

People page No

Index

People continued page No

Places

Index

English Tribes

Essex Hundred Publications

Once Upon a time in Southend (and District)

Cartoons are one of the most popular staples of newspapers. The cartoonists' genius lies not just with drawing skills but their ability to bring together contemporary and historical events in a single image.

ISBN 9780993108396 £9.99

BATTLEFIELD ESSEX

2000 years of conflict in Essex

ISBN 9780993108341 £9.99

THE ESSEX HUNDRED HISTORIES

From the Roman sacking of Colchester to Ford's modern day wind turbines each chapter reflects the diversity of the county as well as showing the role Essex has played in the nation's development. (reprinted 14 times)

ISBN: 9780993108310 £9.99

THE ESSEX HUNDRED

The history of the county of Essex described in 100 poems and supported with historical notes and illustrations.
A unique book written by Essex poets covering 2,000 years of county history.

ISBN: 9780955229503 £7.99

LONDON'S METROPOLITAN ESSEX

Events and Personalities, from Essex in London, which shaped the nation's history.

ISBN 9780955229558 £12.99

THEY DID THEIR DUTY, ESSEX FARM
Never Forgotten

A book that tells the story of Essex Farm, a First World War cemetery in Belgium, that will forever bear the county name, and its connections to the Essex Regiment.

ISBN 9780955229596 RRP £9.99

THE ESSEX HUNDRED CHILDREN'S COLOURING AND ACTIVITY BOOK

The Colouring and Activity Book is another title from the Essex Hundred family aimed at children and part written by children. The book includes not only Essex information but pictures to colour in, word searches, puzzles and questions.

ISBN: 9780955229534 £4.99

THE NUMBERS HAD TO TALLY

by Kazimierz Szmauz

A World War II Extraordinary Tale of Survival

ISBN: 9780955229572 RRP £8.99

Buffalo Bill's Wild West

by David Dunford

The First Reality Show in Essex

The extraordinary story of Buffalo Bill, his Wild West show and what happened when they came to Essex in the early 1900s.

ISBN 9780993108389 £8.99

MAGNA CARTA IN ESSEX

Essex barons were at the forefront of those who pushed hard for the Magna Carta, with Robert Fitzwalter, Lord of Dunmow appointed their leader. Yet within three months of the charter being sealed England was at war and Essex racked by conflict.

ISBN 9780993108303 £7.99

Digital Editions available

Essex Farm
The Numbers Had to Tally
L33 and other stories from WWI

Essex Hundred Publications publishes a range of Essex centred local history books. By Essex we mean not just the county of Essex as it is today but also the areas of Essex that have been absorbed into London since 1965. The company also distributes a range of local history books from other publishers and has a large portfolio of Essex images.

Essex Hundred authors are also happy to give talks on the subjects published. For further details consult www.essex100.com or e-mail ask@essex100.com

Essex Hundred Publications

Books written, designed and printed in Essex.
Available from bookshops, book wholesalers,
direct from the publisher or
online www.essex100.com